THE BOYS CLUB

HOW CHILDHOOD TRAUMA TRAPS SOME MEN INTO CHILD-LIKE BEHAVIORS

DR. WAYNE A. BECKLES, LCSW-C

2019

Copyright © 2019 Dr. Wayne Beckles.

Printed in the United States of America on acid-free paper.

All rights reserved. No part of this book may be reproduced or transmitted in any means or form by any electronic or mechanical including photocopying and recording, or by any information storage and retrieval system.

ISBN-13: 978-0-359-99595-0 (Paperback Edition)

Beckles, Wayne.
The Boys Club, How Childhood Trauma Traps Some Men into Child-like Behaviors.

Library of Congress Cataloging-in-Publication Data.
p.cm.
(alk. paper)

Cover Photograph by Andre Nolan Beckles.
Book design and typesetting by Nikiea.

Printed in the United States of America.

Visit www.drwaynebeckles.com.

Dedication

This is for the men who did not know any better...

And for the ones who knew better, and chose differently...

This is for the men who did not know they were angry...

This is for the men who could not name their emotion, but were still controlled by it...

This is for the men who were raised to "never put their hands on a woman..."

This is for the men who did not fully realize what they were doing until it was too late...

...and they had already swung the fist, pushed, grabbed, choked, or in some other way hurt someone that they said they...loved.

This is for my sons and grandson...for my daughter and granddaughters...may you all learn to resonate at the Bliss Level of emotional awareness and experience the Principle of Thrive while you are here on earth.

TABLE OF CONTENTS

The Little Black Book	pg. 1
A Wolf In Sheep's Clothing	pg. 11
Sex, Porn, And Video Games	pg. 23
Trolling Narcotics Anonymous	pg. 39
Spider Manic!	pg. 49
Love Sick	pg. 63
Collateral Damage	pg. 69
Training Camp	pg. 81
The Alley Man	pg. 97
The Antidote	pg. 113

conversation peace

Not

Right now

I don't want

To talk about it

I can't talk about it

I do not yet even fully

understand what "it" is.

I can't get it off my chest

'cause it is still knotted up

in my stomach. I don't know

why I am so mad, if anger is

what this is. I don't want

to talk to you. I don't

need you to talk to me.

I just need to

get lost in

you.

Beckles (1996)

Introduction

Several years ago, I wrote *Crossing the Desert: One Man's Journey From Emotional Mutism and Life in Exile to Becoming Whole* (2006). That book catalogued several of the experiences which contributed to what I refer to as the cracks in the arc of my personal evolution. I came to realize that I was once what Robert Bly refers to in his book, *Iron John* (2004) as a naïve man. I was stuck in a cycle of repeating a pattern of destruction, pain, hurt, and self-sabotage. I believed that there was little to nothing I could do about it.

I learned how to fight, and fighting was associated with surviving. Fighting became my modus operandi and then it was what would manifest in all emotionally stimulating situations. Other emotions like fear, hurt, or vulnerability did not get to fully form, or become recognizable viable options. There was only anger and fighting.

Bly goes on to say that "a spiritual man may love light, and yet be entirely numb in the chest area [because he] decided to have no feelings at all." Bly adds that he felt that "as a man gets older, certain numb parts of his body naturally begin to come to life." I raise a word of caution here. I am concerned that for many men, this process is not "natural" nor is it automatic as Bly would seem to suggest. A primary reason for writing *The Boys Club* is that I have encountered far too many men and the women and children who are the collateral victims of those men who fail to do their work to evolve, to think it is enough to let nature take its course.

For many men, parts of their emotional development remain stuck at an age prior to full adult. They may be doctors, lawyers, policemen, firemen, CEOs, or even, President. They may be able to pay bills, balance budgets, or run corporations. They may even be good husbands and fathers. But still there may be something missing. This thing that is missing shows up as an ache, a yearning, a call that comes from the soul of the world that they hear but cannot answer.

For these men, they are stuck at point on their personal evolution that renders them unable to have a fully adult emotional experience of, and response to emotional stimuli. Aspects of their emotional maturity remain stunted, whether by trauma or some other factor that impedes their development. As a result, the age of their emotional mindset might be closer to six or eight, while in every other sense, they are full grown men. Throughout my life, these men have shown up in different forms and their wounded little boy is sitting there, just beneath the surface.

This book serves as a discussion of these intersecting topics and explores how both childhood trauma and factors in our socialization result in unhealthy behaviors in adult males. I deepened the inquiry after I saw some striking patterns among my male clients. This book is intended to shed some light into the substance of those findings. I am writing this book so that current and future generations of boys can grow into fully emotionally mature adult men.

My work focuses on helping my clients to move along the emotional continuum from emotional mutism to emotional fluency; to create practices to regularly access the Bliss Level of emotional vibration and to activate the Principle of Thrive for themselves and those around them.

AUTHOR'S NOTE

All of the cases described in this book are composites. They have been intentionally scrambled in order to protect the privacy rights and confidentiality of my clients. Any similarity to any persons, living or dead, is purely coincidental. I have noticed that the lyrics to many popular songs reflect men struggling with or celebrating the concept of promiscuity. Throughout the book, I have made an attempt to interlace excerpts from these songs, which reflect a cultural value for cheating.

THE BOYS CLUB

HOW CHILDHOOD TRAUMA TRAPS SOME MEN INTO CHILD-LIKE BEHAVIORS

CHAPTER ONE

THE LITTLE BLACK BOOK

It was a sunny autumn day. My wife and I were stopping at the local post office to finalize arrangements for our relocation to a small town in rural Maryland. As we stepped out of our car, we were stunned to recognize the face of the woman sitting in the car next to us. We thought we were far away from everything and everyone in our past. We desperately needed a fresh start and thought we had selected a place where we would not know a soul. Don't get me wrong, we were happy to see her, just not expecting to see her there. How lucky we felt to see a familiar face. Little did we know what would unfold in the next few seconds.

"Jocelyn!" We called out. She looked up, apparently as surprised as we were. She got out of her car and the three of us embraced. We explained that we were about to move to this town. When we asked her what she was doing there, she barely got out the words: "I escaped" before bursting into tears. Between her sobs, she was able to say: *"I found his little black book. I had no idea he was such a monster!"*

Jocelyn went on to pull out of her pocket a tattered photocopy of a page from the book that she said she kept with her as a constant reminder of how methodical her ex-boyfriend, Darryl, was and how he reduced women to statistics in the way that that people do when they play fantasy football. This was a game for him and in the process, he was destroying women's lives. She wanted to make sure that she would always keep her guard up and never again get seduced by his sweet talk.

She shared with us the image she held in her hand:

Name:	J. B.
Nickname:	D.H.C.
Type:	Earthy/Hippie Chick
Met:	Farmer's Market
Dates:	June 8, 2012
Bagged:	September 4, 2012 at 4:30 PM living room couch of parent's house.
Love Lang.	Acts of Service
Fav. Color:	Key Lime Green
Fav. Song:	You Don't Know My Name by Alicia Keys
Panty Type:	Thongs
Sex position:	Missionary with eye contact
Rating:	5 out of 10 stars but can be groomed

"This was my page!" Jocelyn exclaimed. "I used to be upset that he only rated me as a 5! Now, I'm so ashamed! I can't believe that I even worried about that. I'm here thinking that he loved me, but it was more like I was a thing! His nickname for me was DHC!"

My wife asked what that stood for and Jocelyn replied that it was short for Dumb House Cat!

My wife asked suspiciously: "How did you know that?"

Jocelyn replied that when they argued, he would call her that to her face.

Incredulous now, my wife asked: "And you stayed?"

Jocelyn replied: "I felt trapped." She continued: "It was not always this way. It started off really nice. He was sweet and took care of everything I needed. Now I realized that he was slowly getting me to let my guard down. Then he started boxing me in by alternating the compliments with criticism by saying things like: *You are not humble enough…You are not a ten. You're average looking and fat!* It took me lots of therapy to understand that he was playing on my insecurities."

After a pause, Jocelyn continued: "He even had details of how he talked me into giving up my car and stopped me from seeing my family…(sobbing) I thought it was something special to have him invite me to live with him and help him build his company-but I was really just his prisoner! All those so-called business meetings were really hook ups with other women!"

Jocelyn continued: "Then in stage three, when I said I wanted to leave, he was making me believe that I was not ever going to be any good to anyone, even myself! Every time he did something wrong, he would yell and make it seem like it was my fault."

My wife asked: "What did he say when you told him that you were leaving and why?"

Jocelyn replied: "Oh, I did not tell him right away. I knew what would happen if he thought I went through his stuff. I waited until the next day, then called my cousin after he went to work. She was there in an hour and while I waited for her, I packed my stuff. She wanted to destroy the place, but I knew what he would do to me if that happened."

I interjected: "You keep saying that. What would he have done?"

Jocelyn responded by stating: "He has this other side that is so scary. There were a few times when I disagreed with him and he got so mad, I thought he was going to kill me."

After pausing to collect herself, Jocelyn continued: "There were these times when we would fight, and he would hit me. Then when I went to talk about it the next day, he would say it never happened. It got so bad that I got one of those Nanny Cams and left it running in the living room. Soon after that we had one of those fights and the next day when I showed him the video, he started crying and said that he "blacked out" and did not remember any of the things that were on the video."

"I know it kills him to think he could do this because he lives and dies by the notion that he is a perfect gentleman and he swears he would never put his hands on a woman. The funny thing is the words he would say to me were much worse than the times he hit me. In a way, I am so glad I found that book, because if I hadn't, I would probably still be there working like his slave. I cried that entire day because it hurt so much."

Jocelyn paused, then continued: "The way he would control my mind was the scariest. I thought I was stronger than that, but he would say and do these things that left me questioning my own sanity. I would catch him red-handed doing some bullshit and next thing I know he had me questioning what I know I saw and apologizing to him for offending him with the accusation. How crazy is that?"

"So, weren't you afraid he would come after you?" I asked.

My wife asked: "Did you ever call the cops?"

Jocelyn: "Please! I tried to get a restraining order and the police even said that those things are only as good as the paper they are written on and that paper cannot stop a fist or a bullet. My family decided that we had to come up with our own insurance policy."

Jocelyn continued: "My cousin helped me a lot. She has some friends who are police officers. They helped me get a restraining order and before we left, she helped me to put together this note saying that I made copies of his black book and that I would have three people publish the photocopies of it if he ever contacted me again or if anything ever happened to me."

I asked: "Have you ever heard from him again?"

Jocelyn replied: "He tried contacting me a few times and he showed up at my parent's house, but I was able to stay invisible for a while until he seemed to stop looking for me. He has moved on now. My cousin ghost follows him on social media and every once-in-a-while we look at his status. It seems like he has found a perfect host bride to live off. She is this really pretty woman that works in broadcasting—I think she does the weather or something. They are married and he is living well off of her money. I am sure he is up to the same old shit and she does not have a clue."

My wife asked: "You ever think about contacting her to warn her?"

Jocelyn stated: "My cousin asked me that a few times, but I made her promise that all we would do is stalk him on social media but never get back into that world at all. I am glad I got out and never want to reconnect with anything to do with him again."

Jocelyn's story had me mesmerized. I felt like I knew Darryl my entire life and wondered how I could have missed all of this. It made me re-think all of my experiences with him. Growing up…Darryl Ray was the coolest kid I knew. I recall that when we were still in elementary school, he articulated that he had a goal to have sex with women from every different nationality. As an impressionable elementary school kid, I thought that this quest was admirable.

It was not until we were older that I began to learn

the truth about him. He presented a persona of the *perfect gentleman*, but underneath, he was everything other than that. I learned that he did not even use his real last name. It appears that his deceased father had some illegal dealings as a result, the family went under a modified name to conceal their identities.

I thought of this kid as my best friend at that time and actually felt lucky that he would allow me to be his friend. I wanted to do everything I could to impress him and bought him a gift of a velvet poster of a black panther (which seemed so cool in the early 1970's). I emptied my piggy bank and took all of my loot to the corner store to buy this gift for my bestie.

Since I took pennies, nickels, and dimes to the store for my purchase, my change was given back to me in pennies. I wanted to show that all my money was presented to my friend for his happiness on his birthday, so I placed the remaining pennies into the plastic wrap that made a tube for the poster. For a kid from a really, really poor country, I did not anticipate the offense that my friend would experience by receiving pennies as a "gift." He threw the fistful of pennies onto the floor in disgust. I was left hurt and confused by the whole incident.

I moved to Long Island a few years later and Darryl and I maintained sporadic contact throughout our high school and college years. One year, when I was back in Queens for the summer, I bumped into my friend while I was on my way to visit my cousin in Brooklyn. He said that he was on his way to see his girlfriend in another part of Queens and since we were both traveling in the same direction, we might as well travel together and hang out afterwards. I have to admit that I was still not over the influence of his very charming, charismatic persona.

After we visited his very sweet and extremely good-looking girlfriend in the Astoria section of Queens, we hopped on the train to the East New York section of Brooklyn. I realized that he was flirting with my cousin and got her number, but because of my values at that time, I actually thought that his womanizing was cool. I later learned from my cousin that they began dating immediately after that initial encounter.

Many years later, my cousin would tell me that he was also physically abusive to her. She would also go on to explain that she learned from his mother that this was precisely the behavior that his father displayed in the house, when Darryl was growing up. Darryl's mother revealed that there were times that she was even afraid of what Darryl would do during his violent rages. I had no idea that this was a foreshadowing of a pattern of behavior that I would learn about in vivid details a dozen years later.

After completing school and working for three years, I got laid off. I had been the sole breadwinner. My wife and I had a two-year-old and our second child was just two-months old at the time. We decided to move in with her parents while I continued to look for work where I had the most promising job leads. I spent the weeks looking for work in the D.C. area, while sleeping on my friend Darryl's couch and commuting to spend the weekends with my family on Long Island. Within a couple of months, I secured employment, got an apartment, and was able to have my family join me in our new town.

It felt like natural chemistry for my wife and I to hang out with Darryl and his girlfriend, Jocelyn. However, with two small children, it proved difficult to keep up with the social calendar of a young couple with no kids. We eventually drifted apart. Both my wife and I were stunned to learn what became of the couple we once thought we knew so well.

CHAPTER TWO

A WOLF IN SHEEP'S CLOTHING

>hoping for the arms of mater
>strangled by the wishes of pater
>
>*Holding Back the Years by Hucknall, M. & Moss, N. (1985).*

Carl Chang was referred to me through the Employee Assistance Program (EAP), provided by his local precinct. He had been placed on administrative leave and was not able to perform his regular police duties, wear his badge or carry his gun. He was being investigated for the charges associated with his most recent offense.

Carl had several previous problems during his employment with his precinct. In one incident, he was reprimanded by his supervisor because of a hit and run incident that he did not report. The accident was viewed on security camera in the parking garage of his police precinct. Carl was seen backing into the personal vehicle of one of his fellow officers. Additionally, Carl got into trouble for failing to respond to a call because he was asleep in his cruiser and did not hear the radio. However, these incidents did not come close to the level of severity of his last offense.

On the night in question, Carl radioed in that he was pursuing a car for speeding on the local boulevard, within his jurisdiction. Thirty minutes later, he was when radioed to respond to suspicious activity within his jurisdiction, it was noted in the dispatcher's log that he did not respond to the call. The dispatcher also noted in the log that Carl did not call in to "clear" his prior report that he was apprehending a vehicle for speeding. It is worth noting that these calls are usually cleared within five to ten minutes, so it is unusual for an officer to not have cleared a call for more than thirty minutes.

When Carl re-established radio contact with the dispatcher, he indicated that he had gone on his break after pulling over the car for speeding, but forgot to radio it in. It was not until the next morning that it was discovered what actually happened during the thirty minutes that Carl was not in communication with the precinct dispatcher. A 32-year old African American woman went into a neighboring police precinct to report that she was raped by a uniformed police officer, after she was pulled over for speeding the night before.

The woman reported that she was driving a vehicle that fit the description of the car that Carl reported pursuing for speeding, gave a description of the officer, which bore a strong resemblance to Carl Chang, and reported Carl's badge number, which she memorized as he raped her. The woman reported one other detail that she thought was bizarre, she stated that the officer folded his jacket and placed it under her rear, stating he wanted her to be comfortable. The woman stated that she was confused by this action because it made her wonder if he did not realize that he had drawn his service revolver and it was impossible for her to be "comfortable" while being raped at gunpoint.

During the initial session of the evaluation, Carl was happy to point out that he knew something about psychology and reported that he took an online personality test and learned that his enneagram was a 6: Loyalist. He added that he "felt at home" with this enneagram as it seemed to accurately describe him and helped him to understand a few things that he was not fully clear about, like why he was always accused of being obsessed with order, right and wrong and compliance.

Carl had attempted to join several police departments in the past but was repeatedly rejected because he failed the psychological portion of the exam. After several years of trying, Carl was able to gain acceptance to the ranks of the city police department. It is unclear if this was because the local police department did not administer a psychological exam, or if they did, nobody checked Carl's results before offering him a position on the force. What is clear, however, is that the reasons that showed Carl would not be a suitable candidate for the other police departments that denied him entry, were also reasons why he should not have gained entry to the police department where he was employed, as well.

There are aspects of Carl's personality that would make him fail the psychological exam for they reveal that he lacks several of the characteristics that would make for a good law enforcement professional. Moreover, there are several other personality deficits which indicate that Carl was likely to use the power afforded to him in his position as a police officer, to overcompensate for these deficits. Not only did Carl lack some fundamental skills necessary for effectively carrying out the duties of a police officer, but his personality deficits indicated that it was just a matter of time until the ticking time bomb, exploded.

In essence, Carl's personality deficits meant that it would be only a matter of time before he was involved in a violent incident triggered by his fear. While one person would be able to effectively de-escalate the situation, Carl's psychological profile would suggest that when faced with a tense confrontation, he was more likely to panic and act out irrationally, than to defuse the situation.

Carl posed somewhat of a diagnostic challenge to me. He possessed the feelings of inadequacy and avoidance of social interaction (despite a strong desire for intimacy) that is customarily associated with Avoidant Personality Disorder. Carl also possessed the difficulty in decision making and psychological dependence on others that is associated with the Dependent Personality Disorder.

However, his choice of a career in public service seemed incongruent with his meeting all of the criteria for either one of the above diagnoses. By Carl's self-report, his attitudes towards men in authority tended to be conforming and submissive. In contrast, when it came to women in positions of authority (or otherwise) Carl's attitudes tended to be hostile and aggressive.

A discussion with Carl about his early childhood experiences shed plenty light onto how Carl came to be the way he is. Carl was the only child born to the unwed union of his parents, who were both Chinese immigrants. When he was younger, Carl reports that he was a "mousey and undersized boy." He was considered the "runt of the litter" in his extended family. He had trouble asserting himself and stuttered badly as a child.

Carl's background included being raised in a strict "hell fire and brimstone" religious household where his mother was a particularly domineering enforcer of all the rules, particularly those with which she could quote chapter and verse from the bible for her references.

Carl reported that he lived in a house with his grandmother and for the first ten years of his life, he believed that she was his mother. He reported that there was a woman who lived at a separate residence and would visit periodically. Carl added: "I was told that she was my aunt and that is how I interacted with her and what I called her. It was not until my tenth birthday that my "aunt" showed up with this man who had gifts for me. I did not know who he was, but they explained to me that he was my father, the woman I thought was my aunt was my mother, and the woman I thought was my mother was her mother."

Carl reported that everything changed on that day. "I hated all of the adults in my life!" He added that before that day, "I used to call my grandmother mommy and I called my mother, my aunt." This was at the same time that I had to move with my grandmother into a house with my mother. This was all so strange to me. New house, new family structure, and most of all so many lies that they told me.

I was told that I would have to change my last name to his, but that did not feel right. Carl reported that his father did not join them in the family residence, and he had limited contact with his father after meeting him on his tenth birthday. The hardest part was suddenly having a father show up and then not stay. Carl went on to say: "I felt like my father never claimed me as his own." Carl reported that he tried to do well in school and in sports, etc. but nothing made his father come around. Carl concluded: "There was nothing I could do that would ever be enough for him."

When Carl was relating his experiences as an adult, he had disclosed that he had repeatedly gotten stuck at Step #8 of his 12-Step recovery process, which required him to make amends. He was describing the situation where he was being confronted by his stepdaughter (whom he had molested when she was between 9 and 11 years old). He reported that he had been invited to meet with her in therapy but surprised to see that she was accompanied by her therapist and her mother.

During his discussion with me about that therapeutic confrontation, he repeatedly said "I took responsibility for what I did, but she had all the power." It was only after much prodding, that I came to realize that Carl merging the stepdaughter that he abused—who at the moment of his being held to account for his molestation in therapy, when bolstered by her mother and therapist, became powerful—had been merged in his psyche with his mother (who for him had always been the all-powerful "she.") In that moment of his taking responsibility he crossed the line between perpetrator and victim. I realized that this was the reason why he was continually getting stuck at step #8. Making amends would be extremely difficult, if you feel like you are the aggrieved party.

Although Carl took his aggression out on women, it was revealed in therapy that he held deep-seeded animosity towards his father. He also felt a great deal of disappointment in himself because as the first born son in an Asian family, he had a certain obligation to honor. He blamed himself for his father's absence. Carl once said: "I am going to win the brass ring and give it to my father." When asked to clarify that statement, Carl simply said, that he wanted to prove himself worthy in his father's eyes.

Carl was eager to discuss his dating experiences (or lack thereof) with me. It seems as if he felt that by being able to state his case about how he had been wronged during his experiences with women, he could somehow justify his behaviors. Normally I would begin my assessment with trying to get background information regarding my client's childhood. However, in this instance, my client was so forthcoming with details regarding his adult experiences that seemed to relate to his crime, I elected to stay on this line of questioning and elicit as much detail as was relevant. Carl mentioned that in his most recent dating relationship, which ended two years prior he had become romantically involved with a woman who used him for his money.

WB: Can you tell me about the events that led up to your getting arrested?

CC: I came home from work and found my roommate having sex with her cousin on the couch.

WB: How did that involve you?

CC: I was attracted to her and she knew I wanted to have a physical relationship with her. She told me that she wanted to take a break and get her head together before getting into a sexual relationship. But she was lying to get to keep staying in my apartment for free. I even let her use my car, when she did not have a way to get around to look for work. I bent over backwards for her and all she wanted to do was use me. Now that she is back on her feet, she acts like I do not exist. This is the shit that happens all of the time. I am sick of it.

WB: Has something like this happened before?

CC: Yes. Women don't really want to date me. They prefer to use me.

WB: You seem to have some pretty solid ideas about

women and how they will treat you. When did you first start thinking this way?

CC: I have always been shy and awkward around the ladies. I'm not the kind of guy that women say 'yes' to.

WB: Tell me more about that.

CC: I have had experiences where women have looked at me with a glint in their eye and a little smile on the corner of their mouth. As soon as we say hello and shake hands, that smile is gone, and the conversation is over. I am not sure what it is, but they seem to know from 'hello' that I am not their type. I kept believing that I was gonna win the brass ring and bring it to my dad and show him that I was good enough to win the brass ring (and good enough for him to love me…).

After that, I kinda gave up trying to deal with women directly. I thought about getting one of those mail-order brides, but they all seem to be trying to get you to send them money before you even meet them. That feels like I am being used all over again. Besides, you don't even know if it is really the person, or if their sob story is even true. You could be getting catfished.

Carl reported that because of his insecurity and fear of being rejected by women he wanted to date, he would use Facebook and LinkedIn to become "friends" with women that he would not normally be able to say hello to if he met them in person. He added that he would often use the websites to try to determine if the women were in a relationship or single. When it appears that the women are single, he would try to make it appear as if they have something in common by pretending to be interested in the things they like and to make comments on their posts. He admitted that he knew that his behavior bordered on stalking.

What was revealed from Carl's evaluation was that he scored high on the measures for repressed anger, significant hostility towards women, and discomfort with asserting himself. Carl had previously described his father as a passive weakling and stated that the parts he hates about himself, are the parts that remind him of his father. Carl also reported being bullied extensively at school and stated that a secret motivation for becoming a police officer was so that he could get revenge on the people who bullied him. He stated that he always wanted to be a police officer, and no one was surprised by his desire to do so. Carl reported that he excelled at being a cub scout, a boy scout, and a police explorer.

There is a subsection of the men I work with who use pornography and video games as an outlet which allows them to embrace an aspect of their personalities that they do not feel they can otherwise express. I go into more detail about these men in my chapter entitled: Porn, Sex, and Video Games. One of my other clients stated that he felt this was perfectly acceptable because it allowed him to be violent in a safe space where no one got hurt and he did not have to face any consequences. It is as if their alter egos are free to reign over their imaginary kingdoms in the safe space of a parallel universe. Carl reminds me of those men, with one significant distinction. Carl's alter ego does not have a parallel universe and any damage that it causes, occurs in this universe with real victims.

It is a relief that Carl was found guilty and sentenced for his crime. He posed a particularly scary threat to society. Carl's gun and badge gave him entrée to a level of false confidence and despite lacking a stable sense of self-esteem, Carl's ego was propped up by the notion that people would respect the uniform and he could say things to women that he would not dare to utter "in real life." The problem was, that this is real life and his combination of factors would result in a series of games of cosplay with very real and very dangerous, if not fatal, consequences.

CHAPTER THREE

Sex, Porn, & Video Games

> Why must I feel like that?
> Why must I chase the cat?
> Nothing but the dog in me...
> *Atomic Dog by George Clinton (1982)*

In his seminal work, *Soul Murder: The Effects of Childhood Abuse and Deprivation*, Leonard Shengold asserted that:

Soul murder involves the deliberate traumatization or deprivation by an authority (parent) of his charge (child). The victim is robbed of his identity and of the ability to maintain authentic feelings. Soul murder remains effective if the capacity to think and to know has been sufficiently interfered with--by way of brainwashing....The need to identify with and to maintain the illusion of a good parent enforces the difficult resistance of denial (brainwashing becomes self-enforced) (1989).

Shengold makes an excellent argument about the impact of what I call the problems associated with too much or too little. The abuse would be too much exposure to the things that are not meant for children and the neglect would be too little exposure to the things that are necessary for children to experience as part of their healthy development. In this chapter I will cast two very different profiles which reflect the deliberate traumatization of too much and the deliberate deprivation of too little and how the too much and too little have contributed the manifestation of addictive behaviors of a subset of the adult men with whom I have worked.

Although the experiences of the men are vastly different, they somehow converge in a pool of sex-related addictive behaviors. On one hand, some of my clients struggle to repress (or control) the behaviors and to see themselves as "good" people being tempted by "bad" things. They feel tremendous guilt and shame when they succumb to temptations. On the other hand, for others, there is no struggle, no guilt, and no shame. Their only problem is the consequence and dealing with the ramifications of getting caught (these look more like the profile I discussed in the first chapter of this book entitled: *The Little Black Book*).

My first profile of this chapter I will call Micah W. He is a 34-year old Hispanic man. He is a single parent with 4 children from 4 different women ranging in age from 18 to 8. He stated that he was not allowed to have contact with his eldest child, nor her mother because of his past abusive behavior towards the child's mother.

He reports having civil relationships with the mothers of his three other children. He noted that the mother of his 12-year-old son was killed when she was hit by a stray bullet during a gang-related shoot-out in her neighborhood several years ago. He was then granted full custody of their son.

Micah initially came in to see me a few years ago in the weeks leading up to Christmas. He was referred for outpatient therapy after being discharged from the local hospital where he was evaluated because he was "not thinking clearly." He later admitted that "not thinking clearly" meant that he was entertaining thoughts of harming himself which is what led to his need for a psychiatric evaluation.

Micah reported that his reason for seeking therapy was because he was having relationship problems with his fiancée after being together for 10 years and it has put a tremendous mental strain on him. He continued by stating that the relationship problems and stress from work became too much for him and caused things to begin to unravel.

Micah initially stated that the source of friction in the relationship is the way his fiancée's children treat his children. Micah later revealed that another underlying reason for the conflict he experienced in his relationship with his fiancée was that he refused to put her name on the deed to the house (which he claimed to have bought for both of them and their children).

Afterwards, Micah confessed that the real reason that he and his fiancée are having problems is because she does not trust him and is always accusing him of cheating on her. He quickly added that he does not fully trust her because he feels that she may be using him, and this is the reason why he did not put her name on the deed. When asked about the issue of trust in their relationship, Micah admitted that he was not good at having relationships. He further clarified that although he has had a constant girlfriend or fiancée for the past 17 years, he has never been faithful to any of them.

When asked if problems with trust existed for him in any prior relationships, Micah was quick to say that he has always had trouble with trust, as it was damaged early for him because the people who he depended on and trusted to protect him, violated that trust. When exploring this violation of trust, the following dialogue ensued:

WB: Can you give me some instances of how that trust was violated?

MW: I remember, when I was a kid, they sent me next door to eat pussy.

WB: How old were you?

MW: About six or seven.

WB: What was your reaction to that?

MW: It was strange. I can remember seeing my neighbor's bush. I really did not know what I was doing.

WB: How do you think that impacted you?

MW: I don't know. When I was a little older, I realized I had more experience than the other boys my age, so it felt kinda cool, but...

WB: But, what?

MW: I have done things with men.

WB: Okay...

MW: Don't get me wrong, I am not gay or anything.

WB: Okay...

MW: I have been with a lot of women.

WB: How many?

MW: So many, I have lost count.

WB: Estimate.

MW: Record breaking...I'm really not sure. (the smile on his face barely masking the shame of knowing that I knew he was trying to prove something that he could not prove).

WB: More than 5,000?

MW: No! Way less than that.

WB: Less than 10?

MW: Way more than that.

WB: Give me a number.

MW: Over 100.

WB: More than 300?

MW: Between 100 and 200. But I can't remember all of them. My self-esteem was a lot lower back then. I would hit that just to make myself feel good. But right after sex, I would start to feel shitty again.

WB: What was your motivation in all of that?

MW: Getting my feelings hurt would make me want to go out and get pleasure from a woman. When it comes to women, I cannot say no. I think I might be a sex addict. Actually, I think both of my parents were sex addicts.

As my therapy sessions continued with Micah, his trust in me as a therapist deepened, and his willingness to disclose expanded. Eventually, Micah was able to share with me that he had been ritualistically sexually abused by his older male cousin between the ages of 7 and 11. He stated that he was threatened that if he told he would die and his mother would be burned alive. reported that he was so fearfulof anything happening, that he elected to not tell anyone and instead would act out. His ways of acting out included running into the street and laying down in the middle of the road, hoping to get run over by a car. He also reported that he would frequently start fistfights with bigger boys at school and cry out in distress that he wished he were dead.

Micah reflected tearfully on this time in his life and explained that he was placed on "the mental ward" about ten different times during this period. He recalled that he was always in distress when he got there but soon afterwards, he missed his family and wanted to go back home, stating it felt good to be out of distress, but bad to be away from home. Micah then disclosed that the most difficult part of the entire ordeal is that his mother did not know what was happening to her own son.

He reported that his mother dismissed his behavior as "acting out" because he wanted more attention after his cousin moved in and was living with them. It was not until he had trouble sitting in school one day after a particularly brutal molestation, that his teacher suspected something. His teacher contacted Child Protective Services who conducted an investigation and determined that Micah was being molested and removed him from the household.

Micah stated that when the abuse stopped and he was returned to live with his mother, it was his turn to be the bully. He would still pick fights, but this time with smaller kids, to ensure that he won the fight. He hoped that his acting wild would intimidate other kids that were his size or bigger. He even wore an extra set of clothes so that no one could see how skinny he actually was. He stated that he put on a persona to show that he was a man because he did not want anyone to take advantage of him the way they did when he was a kid.

Through his preliminary therapy, Micah was able to realize that his anger and his past addiction to substances, as well as his ongoing addiction to sex all stemmed from his childhood trauma. Micah then turned the focus of his ongoing therapy to address his underlying struggles with a sense of self-worth and self-acceptance. He feels that by addressing these issues in therapy he will make headway to resolving his sex addiction. I agree.

> And the cat's in the cradle and the silver spoon,
> Little boy blue and the man on the moon
> When you comin home?
> Son, I don't know when
> We'll get together then
> You know we'll have a good time then
>
> *Cat's in the Cradle by Harry Chapin (1974)*

I will call my second profile Gary J. Gary is a 48-year-old white man. Gary reported that from birth to ten years old, he was raised in a household that was marked with a sense of austerity, a withholding of any of the things that one might enjoy. The most painful thing that was withheld was love. Gary recalled that he lived in a house with a woman he thought was his mother for ten years until she died, and he learned that she was actually his grandmother.

Afterwards, he was placed in an orphanage until they could locate his closest living relative. Gary stated that it was several months before a woman visited him and said she was his mother. She told him that she decided to let his grandmother raise him because that would be a better home for him. She showed pictures from the hospital on the day she gave birth to him. She also showed pictures of her growing up with his grandmother. Finally, she showed a copy of his birth certificate with her name on it to prove that she was who she said she was.

Gary stated that his mother explained that her lifestyle was so chaotic that it was better that her mother raised him. On that day, he came to understand that the woman he had seen in the pictures at his grandmother's house, who he believed to be his aunt, was his mother. She told him that she needed to get some other paperwork together and she would be back for him the next day. Gary, tearfully, related that he waited almost an entire year to see her again.

On his mother's second visit, Gary's biological mother brought him a pack of twinkies and a can of orange soda. She apologized and said that she had gotten into trouble but promised things were going to be better. She reassured him that all she had to do was get the adoption form from her lawyer's office and the orphanage would let her take him home later that day. She told him to pack his things, which he did. He never saw her again.

Gary reported that he realized that while he lived with his grandmother, he was reared with the kind of arms-length type of parenting that someone uses when they don't want you to get hurt. However, when you finally learn the truth, the lie is still a lie and hurts just the same. He felt that his grandmother was overbearing and "ultra-religious" as he put it. He stated that her conservative tendencies led to him having a very restricted set of childhood experiences and since his father was not around, she called on the deacon from their church to assist in his corporal punishment and to teach him how to be a righteous man.

Gary reported that this led to what he feels was "religious abuse." When asked to clarify what that meant, Gary stated that everything was about religion and about austerity and the close regulation of so many common human desires including simple things like food and fun. He claimed that he was fed a constant diet of guilt and shame and the threat that any violation of the strict codes of discipline would be met with the "wrath of God." He reported remembering feeling sometimes like God was out to get him.

Gary stated that: "I think all of the religious repression eventually backfired. My grandmother wanted me to be a man of the cloth, but instead, I became a porn addict. The more they told me it was bad, the more I was curious about it." He continued by stating that one time the staff at the orphanage walked in on him and discovered that he was masturbating. He recalls being shamed for this and that they beat him with a paddle, while quoting the bible.

Gary stated that when he was a kid, he was diagnosed with ADHD. He added that this made him feel like he was dumb and feel like something was wrong with him. He revealed that he has always been quiet and preferred to stay to himself as he experiences a high level of anxiety in social situations. He wondered out loud if the mystery of who his father was and the confusion around who his mother was took a toll on his sense of self. He stated that he felt that things were always subject to change and if he did anything wrong, he would have to face the wrath.

Gary went on to say that his lack of self-confidence also extended into his interactions with girls. He admitted that he was very uncomfortable when it came to interacting with girls. He was afraid to make a mistake, so he was reluctant to say or do anything. He added that he never made the first move and any girlfriend he ever had was not because he picked her, but it was because she picked him.

Gary reported that he was married but is currently divorced. When asked how he selected his wife, Gary laughed and stated: "I don't pick them. They pick me. I'm the type of guy that women would accept when they are in need and reject when things get better for them. I'm the type of guy that women would leave at the altar because they met somebody better on the way to the church."

When asked what all of that meant, Gary clarified that he did not select his wife, either. Stating: "My wife picked me, and I agreed to marry her. I was never good at initiating conversations with girls or women, so I usually talked to whoever talked to me." He stated that the fact that she selected him was consistent with the pattern in his life. He elaborated by saying he did not have trouble meeting women because many women seemed to find him attractive. However, there was always something that turned them off, and he did not know what it was.

Gary went further to say that he once met someone, and he could tell she was interested by the way she said hello and smiled. He then spoke about how disappointed he was to watch the twinkle in her eyes vanish as she turned and walked away after all he did was shake her hand and introduce himself. Gary reported that that type of thing happened so often that he was relieved to meet someone who indicated that she wanted to marry him. Gary added that they did not need to have sex, or even to love each other.

Gary reported that he was selected by an older woman who had two children from previous marriage. He reported that they were kind to one another, but theirs was an asexual relationship and more of a business arrangement than a marriage. She was ten years older and would do everything for him (like cooking, cleaning, and managing his money). In exchange, he would help her with income, manual labor around the house, and childcare, on occasion.

When asked about intimacy in their relationship, Gary said there was none. He added that his ex-wife told him that he was the most emotionally unavailable man she had ever met. He added that she said she should have gotten a clue from their first date. She asked what was his idea of a perfect day, and he described a scenario where he was isolated and left to his thoughts and tinkering the whole time. Gary added that his wife stated that he prefers the company of the people in the videos than people in real life.

Gary indicated that he really enjoyed playing video games because they allowed him to "escape to a parallel universe" where he could connect to a community and be whoever he wanted to be. He added that he really enjoyed role playing games as they let him experiment with roles that were very different from his real life.

Gary went on to clarify that he enjoyed playing video games because they allowed for a level of mastery, instant gratification, and escapism that he could not get in real life. He stated that he enjoyed the life in that parallel universe where he always got to win and it was easier to live there than in regular old-fashioned reality.

When asked about his relationship with porn, Gary revealed that he felt that porn provided a "fix" for him. When pressed for further clarification, Gary stated that he would be mentally stimulated at work, but when he came home, he did not find the same type of engagement. He craved some form of stimulation and found that pleasuring himself to porn provided at least a temporary relief.

Gary became noticeably emotional when talking about the type of porn he prefers to watch. He indicated that he preferred the type of porn that is not hard core. He stated he preferred that type of porn that caters to women and focuses on the relationships and intimacy of the couple. He added that this intimacy is what he felt had really been missing from his relationships and is what he truly craves for his life.

Gary stated that he did not mind having an asexual relationship with his wife because she did not turn him on sexually and the more porn he watched, the less interest he had in his wife. He indicated that he found fetish porn (specifically focused on the feet) most stimulating. When asked if that was an interest he could share with his wife and incorporate into their sexual relationship. He simply said that his wife's feet do not look like the feet of the women in the videos.

He stated that he knew he was in trouble when he noticed that his stepdaughter's feet looked like the ones in the videos. He recalled that at first, he thought it was okay to look at a picture of her feet and fantasize while masturbating. He added that he realized he was spending more and more time being aroused by her feet as she walked around the house barefoot, until one day he crossed the line.

When I asked Gary how he crossed the line, he offered the following response. He stated that he grew close to his wife's children and they enjoyed playing video games with him while he provided childcare if his wife worked an extra shift. He stated that the problem arose when he was home from work for an extended period with a back injury. He would drink along with taking his pain medicine, then play video games and watch porn all day. When his stepdaughter came home from school, they were playing a video game and he talked her into letting him give her a pedicure while she played. He then removed his penis from his shorts and tried to convince her to do the things the women in the video were doing in the porn video that was playing on his cellphone.

Gary stated that he was later arrested and served time for his sex offense. He added that he knows what he did was wrong and that he is remorseful for how he harmed someone who looked up to him and trusted him. He admitted that he ruined everything when he molested his stepdaughter, including his marriage, his family, and his freedom.

Gary stated that he prefers the parallel universe to this one because "in the videos the women don't want you to talk to them. They just do what you tell them and sometimes they do it without your even asking. It's like in those role-playing games. You can be with anybody that you want, and nobody gets hurt."

Gary admits that he knows he falters in his interpersonal interactions and admits that as a result he chooses to spend hours and hours on end, by himself. He stated that he longs for a nurturing supportive relationship, but his anxiety makes the notion of that feel overwhelming to him. He added that since talking was difficult for him, he would prefer to avoid it. However, it is unreasonable to have a relationship that included no talking just having sex, and nothing else. As Gary continued in therapy, the deeper therapeutic work would include spending some time helping him to understand how the interplay of porn, sex, video games, and substance use all stimulated the reward centers of his brain and led to his having more difficulty interacting with real people in real time.

CHAPTER FOUR

TROLLING NARCOTICS ANONYMOUS (NA)

I once heard a story that I thought was so outlandish that the perpetrator must have been a special kind of sinister. It was about a male friend of a female friend of mine who reportedly would sit in Alcoholics Anonymous group sessions and attentively listen to the stories of the women in the group and offer consoling and support. He would use this as a tactic to identify which of those women were the most vulnerable and then try to hit on them.

When I first heard this story, I was angry at the man who would use this place where people go for help as if he were shopping for a date in a "target-rich" environment. I was also angry at the woman who would continue to call this man a 'friend' after learning about how slimy he was.

Several years later, I was in a position to be working as a full-time psychotherapist for a psychiatric practice and two separate female clients told me of their unwillingness to participate in the NA/AA process and their disdain for being in "those rooms" as they were called. While discussing the pros and cons of the 12-step process and finding out what in particular it was that they did not like about those meetings, each client mentioned, among other things, the tendency for some men to use the meetings as an opportunity to prey on vulnerable women. I had chills. Could it be that this behavior is both common practice and common knowledge? All these years later and in two different states, the practice seemed identical.

However, this would turn out not to be the worst-case scenario. I recently had occasion to work with a man I shall refer to simply as, "the Doctor." The Doctor was a strikingly good looking, tall slender African American man, with a muscular build. He had a boyish face and came across as much younger than his actual age of 58. He was referred to see me because he was depressed, anxious and always on alert, which caused him to have trouble sleeping.

During my initial evaluation of the Doctor, he reported experiencing flashbacks where he was confronted with spontaneous memories of traumatic events, and recurrent dreams related to them. He reported feeling a high level of distress associated with his memories. He stated that he was willing to consider doing anything to avoid these distressing memories as they have consumed his thoughts and negatively impacted his mood. He reported feeling on edge all of the time and struggled to avoid acting out in an aggressive manor. He revealed that he seriously considered using again because that was the only thing that seemed to help in the past. However, he knows the consequences of getting high and did not want to engage in any reckless or self-destructive behavior. Instead he decided to seek professional help.

I explained to the Doctor that what he was experiencing are the symptoms that we would normally associate with Post Traumatic Stress Disorder. Upon further exploration, the Doctor revealed that seeing his uncle at his mother's funeral about a month prior to coming in for therapy brought back memories from his childhood and that was when he started to have flashbacks, cold sweats, and panic attacks.

The Doctor reported that at first, he denied that his childhood had anything to do with his adult behavior. In his words, this was based on the notion that, "as a man, I had to take full responsibility for all of my actions, anything else would be less than manly." Your ego makes you want to say that you were in control. This desire to be 'in control' impacted my macho notion that made me think that my childhood experiences had nothing to do with my behavior. But having all of these memories come up after seeing my uncle, makes me feel like there is some kind of connection between what I did and what was done to me." The doctor reported that he wanted to use therapy to explore that connection.

When the Doctor was asked where he wanted to start, he indicated that his memories are more vivid now than ever before and if he did not talk about them now, he fears he would never be able to talk about it. We began by reviewing his childhood trauma.

The Doctor reported that he was born in Alabama, but not raised there. He added that his father passed away when he was five and his mother relocated to live with her mother. He stated that he grew up in a house that included his grandmother his mother, her brother, as well as their children. He was the eldest of his mother's four children, but his uncle had a son and a daughter that were older than he was. The Doctor reported that his childhood was tough as the family was very poor and lived in a rough neighborhood. As a child, the Doctor reported that he had been beaten up by a group of neighborhood boys on multiple occasions and otherwise been exposed to violence on multiple occasions.

The Doctor stated that when he was a child, his mother was physically abusive to him. He stated that she tied him down to his bed, stripped him naked and beat him with a belt, whenever he got into trouble in school. He reported that she said that she did this to keep him humble and to set an example for her younger children.

During a subsequent session, the Doctor reported that he was also a victim of sexual trauma by his uncle which lasted from age 7-10, and he had an older cousin (who is now dead from suicide when he was in his thirties) who would sit next to him on the bed and openly masturbate. The client said he was very young and did not know what to think about his cousin's behavior at the time, but he recalls feeling strange when it went on.

The Doctor added that when he was in his teens, he had been severely depressed and attempted suicide with overdosing with pills twice. He recalls that he did not really know what he was doing. The first time he just got really sleepy for an entire day. The second time, he got severely constipated. He reported that he had briefly considered attempting suicide by hanging himself with a belt, but after witnessing the aftermath of his cousin's suicide (a self-inflicted gunshot to the head) he realized that he would never want to end his life that way.

The Doctor reported that his mother and uncle had both been involved in various typs of criminal behavior and that as he was his mother's oldest male child, he was recruited into the family business early. He added that he was a big boy and his facial hair came in early. He believes he was as young as twelve or thirteen the first time that "my mother began taking me with her as the enforcer during her kleptomaniac binges." He added that he felt this may have been one of the factors that contributed to his ongoing criminal behavior.

The Doctor reported that he was also allowed to get high alongside his mother and uncle and believes that he was about 11 or 12 the first time he smoked pot with them. He indicated that he has tried multiple street drugs in the past including heroin, cocaine, alcohol, and marijuana. The Doctor stated that when he was still getting high, his drugs of choice were cocaine and heroin. The Doctor added that he is happy to say that he has been sober for over twenty years. He is proud to say that he is doing the things that he is supposed to do. He stated that he is doing his "Step Work" in NA to recover from his cocaine and heroin habit of the past.

The Doctor confessed that in the past, he had frequently "faked the funk" when it came to his recovery work. The Doctor told me that he would join neighborhood NA and AA groups and pretend to be in recovery so that he could listen to the stories of the women to identify who he could target for sexual advances.

The Doctor reported that after having some success with "shopping in NA groups" as he put it, he realized that he could use his job to get him regular access to women. He revealed that he viewed the psychiatric ward of the hospital where he worked as a 'fertile hunting ground' to find new prey for his sexual deviance. He used his position as a janitor in the hospital to identify women who were in their most vulnerable state and strategically place himself in a position to have complete control over them while they were in a state of heavy medication. He was clever enough not to risk discovery by assaulting them while they were in the hospital. He calmly seduced them and gained their trust while they were feeling out of sorts.

When asked what happened after they were released from the hospital, he stated that he offered them a place to stay while they were trying to get back onto their feet. He said he would offer to be their doctor in the community and that is how he earned his nickname. In one instance, he offered to help a hospitalized woman to get her car out of the police impound after she was stopped for driving erratically through her town. When the police stopped her, they took her promptly to the ER because she was incoherent.

They towed her car to the impound lot and the fees were accruing daily. He reported that he made her sign over her car to him so that he could get it out of the impound lot. Afterwards he contacted her parents and extorted money out of them by making them buy it back from him for "fair market value!" He added that even after her parents bought her car back, she continued to live with him because she was afraid to leave until he gave her permission.

The doctor reported that "I would have so much control over these women that they would do anything I wanted. They were my sex slaves. I would take whatever I wanted until I was done with them. I would make them move out when I got tired of them or if I found somebody that I liked better. I got so turned on by the power of it all that I would make them sleep with a machete under the pillow as a constant reminder that there was nothing they could do to harm me. It was a way of psychologically torturing them. I felt as though, I could even control their thoughts on the astral plane and even their dreams would be ruled by an awareness of my power."

When asked why he would provide his victims with what could be considered as a weapon, he simply replied that he kept several loaded handguns throughout his residence and let them know that he would never be caught off guard.

He added that he has lost his job and served time for the crimes he has committed but he remains haunted by the lives he has destroyed along the way. He stated that he now feels remorseful about his crimes, while he did not in the past. He reported that step 8 of his NA work which asks him to make amends has become his most difficult step. He has too many victims to count and for most of them he has no idea of how to contact them. He indicated that he would like to use therapy, first to really come clean about all that he has done; second, to heal; and third, to figure out how to pay it forward.

In my thirty-plus year career, I have worked with many individuals who have committed crimes of all varieties. I have interviewed more psychopaths than I care to recall, however, these stories about the systematic predatory grooming and using of these women by the Doctor was particularly troubling. We agreed to collaborate to find ways to help him pay it forward.

CHAPTER FIVE

Spider Manic!

> Sometimes when all the wondering's done
> My heart fills up with sadness
> But then it's back to this race I run
> That most folks would call madness
> *Beckles (1996)*

I can vividly recall the day I met Timmy M. because it was such an unusual day. It was a dreary, slightly overcast afternoon in late May. The temperatures were unusually warm, which seemed to be related to the temporary power outage. While the power was out, the Practice Manager was asked if we would close early due to the blackout. The response was that the clinical staff could move to the window offices on the periphery of the office to take advantage of what little sunlight that was still available and to minimize the losses to the practice. Fortunately, the power returned after about fifteen minutes, and only a portion of the session had to be conducted with makeshift lighting.

Timmy M. arrived in my office early and was sitting patiently in the waiting room when I greeted him. His appearance was striking. He was dressed more like an elderly homeless man than a man in his early twenties. His hair was long and unkempt, looking like it had not been washed in several days. He wore a bizarre ensemble. His clothes were wrinkled, and he combined a mismatch nylon jogging suit with dress shoes and a derby (the type of hat that made by Mr. French look so distinguished when I watched *A Family Affair* on TV as a kid). His breath had that telltale sour smell that emanates from people who have not brushed their teeth yet for the day. His body odor was noticeable. It bore the musty aroma that was indicative of 1-2 days without a shower, and possibly while wearing the same clothes.

Throughout the interview, Timmy had difficulty maintaining eye contact, instead, I would notice him looking at me each time I focused on writing my notes, and quickly look away each time I looked up at him. Periodically during the interview, Timmy would stare off into space and seem to be distracted, with his eyes darting, and even his head occasionally turning to follow something that seemed to suddenly catch his attention. However, when questioned about seeing things, he abruptly denied it.

In other instances, he would struggle, sometimes

unsuccessfully, to stifle a grin or a giggle. When asked about the laughter, he made up a story about "air escaping" from his lungs and continued with saying that a lot of people have been bothered by his laughter but promises that he is not laughing. Timmy stated that on several occasions he got into fights when while he was locked up because people did not understand why he was smiling. He later admitted that he was unable to control his smile, even when he tried.

Timmy's referral listed Schizophrenia. Encountering clients who were experiencing visual hallucinations was not unusual, given the diagnosis. However, all of the previous clients I had seen with this diagnosis were inside of an institution until their symptoms were managed by medication. I was a little taken aback by the way that Timmy interacted with me. He only seemed to be "present" in the room with me for fleeting moments at a time. I was not convinced that his symptoms were being fully managed by his medication.

Timmy had been referred to the practice after being released from a psychiatric hospitalization where he had an Emergency Evaluation after declaring he was going to jump off of a bridge to get away from the spiders that had infested his body. Timmy denied that the referral was accurate and that "everything is just a big misunderstanding because people do not listen and are too quick to jump to conclusions." When asked how it came about that he was admitted for a psychiatric evaluation, Timmy admitted that he evaded police for four days by hiding in the woods subsequent to being pulled over for a road rage incident.

Timmy admitted that he was involved in a fender bender when he drove his car into another vehicle as he was distracted by the spiders inside of his car. Timmy stated that the driver of the other car questioned what he said about spiders and they started to argue. When the police showed up, he drove off. The police arrived at his house later that day looking for him and he ran into the woods. He reported that he planned to stay in hiding until the coast cleared, but the nights began to get too cold to camp out. Soon after emerging from the woods, the police returned to his house and this time, were waiting at the back door when he tried to escape. He was taken for a psychiatric evaluation at the local hospital and ended up being in there for 45 days, because, as he put it: "the police thought I was crazy."

When asked what was it that caused you to get a second psychiatric evaluation, Timmy reported that the second time he was admitted for 5 days because "I needed some space from my step-mother and I wore scrubs and dress shoes to a 'bridge' appointment to say 'fuck you' to the staff and they admitted me because of what I wore". When challenged that he seemed to be minimizing the circumstances of a very serious situation, Timmy reiterated his claim that this was just a big misunderstanding. The following dialogue reflects the conversation I had with Timmy when he tried to convince me that he was of sound mind and that what he was experiencing was based in reality:

WB: Before being sent to the psychiatric hospital, what was going on with you?

TM: Sometimes I am sitting in my room and I see a shadow pass by me... I go into the bathroom and open the medicine cabinet to take my meds, and every once-in-a-while, when I open the cabinet, I see an alternate version of me on the other side copying my behavior.

WB: Are you sure that is not your reflection?

TM: I know it is not my reflection, because I already opened the cabinet. I know this sounds crazy. I just can't figure out why this is happening.

WB: Are there other times things like this have happened and others have told you that it did not happen or that they did not see something that you saw?

TM: Sure. There was this time, two weeks ago, before all this started happening, when I was up pretty late, reading and I heard my grandmother talking to me through the sewing machine she had given me. I told my roommates, and all they did was laugh at me, but I know I heard it.

WB: What did she say?

TM: She was saying stuff like "they're coming" and "go home."

WB: Okay. What else?

TM: I was not sure what that meant, at first, but then it all made sense. There were all these extra people hanging around in Goodwill. I don't think they were even shopping. They were just there moving around in circles. Like in those zombie movies when zombies are huddling around conserving energy, waiting for something to happen. I realized what she was warning me about.

WB: So, help me to understand what she was warning you about.

TM: She was telling me that the government is putting devices into the clothing to track us and control our thoughts and emotions. That is what happens when the clothes go through the "Processing Center" at Goodwill. Those people who were in the store, just huddling around were waiting for processing. They needed to get new clothes with new instructions.

WB: I see. But I still don't understand how this led to you getting to the psychiatric hospital.

TM: Well (sheepishly), when I realized how it was working, I decided that I did not want to be processed or programmed, so I took my clothes off and then I tried to warn the others. I told them they needed to take their clothes off and to get out of there. I guess that's when they called the cops.

WB: What happened then?

TM: I never saw when the cops arrived, but before I knew it, I was naked with handcuffs on, sitting in the back of a police car and they were asking me who I wanted them to call to tell that I was going to have a psychiatric evaluation.

WB: What did you learn from the experience?

TM: I feel like my mind is moving in slow motion.

WB: Tell me more.

TM: It's like it is not working right. I am sitting here listening to you, but I can't even remember what you just said.

WB: Okay. I can repeat the question. What did you learn from the experience?

TM: Sometimes I feel like the FBI was investigating me because I was trying to take out a student loan.

WB: Okay. Say more about that.

TM: "I know that there was a government conspiracy to get money from me"

WB: I see.

TM: They were using my iPhones to track my activities and to control my thoughts. They were making my mind jump from topic to topic to "kill my attention span" and make me think I had ADHD, so that I could be placed on medication.

WB: Sounds like you had a lot going on. Tell me what else was happening at that time.

TM: Well, I started having these crazy mood swings! I would have lots of energy.

WB: Did you ever stay up for a few days at a time?

TM: Nope, but I am tired a lot.

WB: How do you feel today?

TM: Tired.

WB: How much sleep do you get each night?

TM: I don't sleep well. I only get about three hours a night.

WB: How long has this been going on?

TM: For about a year now.

WB: How does this affect you?

TM: I am tired all of the time. This doesn't feel real. It feels like a dream.

    Timmy stated that he feels that he is being tracked through his phone and worries that "Obama can control people making them buy certain things or use electronic waves or paperwork trails." When Timmy was reminded that Mr. Obama was no longer the president, he responded by saying: "I know, but he started this when he was president and is still doing it."

    Timmy stated that he hears the voice of "John Galt" who controls his thoughts and makes him do things against his will. He described this voice as speaking French at times and at other times saying, "go here, see this, do this and it can be yours...". At times the voice tells him to hit someone and makes him feel that if he does this it will give him power. Last week the voice told him to go to Baltimore city and "talk to people." Timmy reported that he did this and states he felt empowered. He believes he has a special gift and is an "Indigo." He believes he is on a special mission to lead a rebellion and "get back at administrators". He reported past suicidal ideation to jump off the Bay Bridge.

Timmy is a 21-year-old single white male whose parents were born in England and emigrated to the United States of America when he was a child. Timmy reported that when he was very young, his mother left the family. He added that soon after that things got very bad. Timmy said that he remembers being always angry because people consistently bullied him because of his British accent. Timmy stated that the ages of 11 through 17 were a very difficult period of his life. He was left to live with his stepmother after his father died and he was completely estranged from the rest of his biological family. Timmy stated that his stepmother would withhold food and affection because he was not her son.

When Timmy was an adolescent, he was placed in a juvenile facility where he was sexually assaulted by one of the older boys. He stated that this has affected functioning and life by always being nervous and shy and being unable to look people in the eye without getting angry. After he got out, he would drink alcohol and smoke marijuana on a daily basis.

Throughout his teens, Timmy reported, that he was dealing with the fallout of that of his mother leaving the family and his being raised by his father and stepmother. Timmy reported his stepmother really stunted him and affected his growth and development and his health. Timmy reported that as a kid he was told he was bright, but the misery had set in and he started not to like anything. Timmy reported that he still feels lost and aimless. He added that he feels he cannot get back what he lost.

Timmy reported that he wishes he never bought that infested car. If he had realized that it was infested with spiders, he would had gotten a different car and avoided all of the trouble this situation with the spiders has caused him. He added that one day when driving, he noticed his friends waving their hands probably trying to get rid of insects. He reported that he cleaned out three spider nests the first week of buying his car.

Since that time, Timmy stated that he has found, four dead spiders in the car, was bitten multiple times by spiders, could feel spiders crawling all over him and sometimes in his food which has caused him to start eating less and decrease the amount of time he slept. He claims that he has lost most of his friends and is unable to have a relationship due to the spider issues. He woke up this morning with a clump of hair on his body (which he believed to be a spider's nest). He stated that his family does not believe him or see the spiders.

He stated that he is very bothered that no one believes him and feels that they've been distancing themselves from him because of their inability to believe what he says. Timmy reported that this has truly become a problem that has affected his functioning and life by causing him to have limited interaction with everyone he knows. Timmy stated that "...people like to throw the word manic around."

Timmy reported that this situation with the spiders

has affected him in all areas of his life. When asked for specifics, he stated that he limits himself from interactions with his friends and family and goes to see a plethora of movies and enjoys laughing and interacting with a group of strangers who are not judging him.

Timmy mentioned that it has also affected his relationship with the mother of his child. He reported that he had been locked up for 3 months for Domestic Violence against her. Upon his release from jail he indicated that they made up and he was able to return to living with her. His girlfriend joined us for one of Timmy's therapy sessions and stated that when he was released from the detention center, he was pleasant, engaging, and optimistic. However, after a few weeks, she reported that Timmy began "acting crazy again." She stated that lately he has been talking to himself, talking really fast and never wanting to stop talking. She also mentioned that he has been very forgetful and cannot seem to make any decisions.

Timmy's girlfriend added that sometimes he gets agitated and aggressive and complains that he feels that people were laughing at him and that his girlfriend could read his thoughts and control his mind. He told his girlfriend he saw 666 on TV and thought that meant that she was demonic. He also said that he could hear the voice of God and felt like he was a prophet.

Timmy stated that he did not think that all of the things that happen to him were symptoms of mental illness. Timmy reported that he believed that some of his experiences (including seeing the "mark of the beast" on

T.V. and "swimming" on the floor in the living room) were part of his spiritual experience. Timmy's girlfriend reported that Timmy told her that his super-powers would be restored if he sold drugs. Timmy denied this allegation.

Timmy reported that his motivation for participating in therapy included his guilt about things that he's done in the past, including hitting his girlfriend and sleeping with men. He stated he wants to make up for those things and be straight so that he could set a good example for his son.

CHAPTER SIX

LOVE SICK

Juan Hernandez is a 22-year old Hispanic male, who is in his senior year in college. He was recently discharged from the psychiatric ward of the local hospital. He had been hospitalized for a psychiatric evaluation after attempting suicide. Juan was being referred to my office for outpatient therapy as part of his hospital discharge plan.

During the initial interview, Juan reported that the emotional issues that resulted in him coming to therapy are anger and depression. Juan feels that his mother showed favoritism to his younger sister. "My one fear of not being good enough fuels my depression." The client's self-report was consistent with that of the diagnostic impression indicated on the referral: "Major Depression Disorder, single episode, moderate and Disruptive Mood Dysregulation Disorder." However, several weeks into his treatment, Juan confessed that he used his brother's name and other identifying information because he feared that if they saw how many times he had been hospitalized in the past, they would place him permanently in the state mental hospital (as had been threatened by his abuela (grandmother).

Juan confessed that the real reason he is in therapy is to work on his anger and depression, but he cannot stop thinking about his relationship issues. He went on to say that he is in a "rollercoaster" relationship with his girlfriend, Lourdes, who he has been dating since high school. He said that they gave their virginity to one another when they were younger, but their relationship has always been intense. He stated that they even had some problems this past week because Lourdes felt like he did not want to talk to her. Juan continued: "with the stuff I went through with my mom, I am not going to let anyone treat me the same way my mom did. One minute you have me on a silver platter and the next minute, I am public enemy number one."

When asked for further clarification, Juan offered: "For a few years, I went to live with my dad, when he got out of prison. Later, I went back home to live with my mother, I felt that my mother began to treat me differently than she treated my sister. That is when I first started feeling sad. I felt like I was a slave in that house." After a long pause, Juan continued: "I want to get myself to a place that, just in case it does not work out with Lourdes, I do not want to get drawn back into my mental black hole."

Juan stated that despite feeling depressed in high school, he was able to do well academically. He began doing poorly in college but thought he would eventually get the hang of it. However, the more he struggled, the worse his anxiety became. His first suicide attempt was by taking a handful of pills during the finals week of his fall semester of sophomore year. He was 19 at the time. As I continued to build rapport with Juan, I was able to learn of his extensive childhood history of psychological abuse by his mother. Juan was originally told that his father was "away at college" and did not learn the truth until many years later.

Juan reported that there was a severe disconnect between he and his mother. He indicated that for significant periods of the eight years that his father was incarcerated, his mother did not have him living with her. Instead, she chose to have him live with her mother. Juan's younger sister had cancer and Juan was sent to live with his grandmother while his sister was receiving chemotherapy. His mother was obsessed with caring for his sister and nothing else. After his sister regained her health, Juan returned to live with his mother, but things were strange. According to Juan, his mother checked out and "forgot about me. All she wanted to do was party and leave me with my grandmother." Juan also reported that he was told by his relatives that his father initially denied paternity and this really hurt him.

Juan stated that he was four when his father went to prison for his involvement in an armed robbery. When Juan's father returned from prison, Juan went to live with him. Juan stated that at first, "I really believed that my father was in school, like they told me, but I eventually figured it out when I was going to visit him one day and I asked my uncle what kind of school it was that did not let you go home. My uncle told me the truth." Juan reported that he began smoking with his father at age twelve and that his father used his contacts to get Juan into strip clubs when he was still underage.

During a subsequent session, Juan reported that an additional motive for coming to therapy is "to show Lourdes that I can change the way I treat her." Additionally, Juan offered that he and Lourdes had a long talk about their relationship, and he told her that he is willing to do his therapy to be able to show that he can change and ultimately get back together with her. When pressed about what precipitated this revelation, Juan revealed that he and Lourdes: "had a little bump in the road."

He and his girlfriend got into an argument about him not wanting her to hear him sing. His girlfriend kept trying to walk off and he continued to try to prevent her from leaving. The situation escalated to the point that Juan grabbed his girlfriend's arm and hurt her as well as ripping her bookbag in an attempt to prevent her from leaving.

Juan admitted that he took these actions out of anger and was attempting to prevent his girlfriend from leaving. Lourdes told Juan that both he and her father get emotional and lash out at her, hurting her feelings in similar ways. Juan stated that this was not the first time they got into physical altercations because of his anger and he worries desperately that she will leave him if he does not change. Juan stated that Lourdes also said that he needs too many things from her.

When pressed about why Lourdes would think something like that, Juan reported that when he is unable to reach her on the phone or feels that she is not showing him the amount of attention and affection that he needs, he is inclined to act out. He exclaimed that his acting out included that he would threaten to harm himself by stabbing himself or crashing his car. He added that there were times where he would refuse to eat, for days at a time. He indicated that he thought Lourdes was the only person who ever truly loved him and that he would want to die if they ever broke up.

Juan was able to understand that because of Lourdes' own emotional history, they were attracted to one another for reasons that were not exactly healthy, in fact, their love was a "sick love." He came to acknowledge that if each person did not do significant work in therapy, they would only create more misery. Juan was able to see that his fear of abandonment that played out in his relationship with Lourdes, stemmed from long before he even met her. He was able to connect the dots to see that his experiences of abandonment as a child led to his neediness and clinging to his girlfriend, and that it was unhealthy. This was the point where his deep therapeutic work began.

CHAPTER SEVEN

Collateral Damage

Selene V. is a 25-year old single white woman who was referred to me for psychotherapy from a local drug rehabilitation program where she received inpatient care after suffering a heroin overdose. Selene reported a history of substance abuse problems beginning at age 11 and lasting for 14 years, culminating in the heroin overdose which caused her to be hospitalized.

When Selene first arrived in my office, she was tense, sullen and appeared to be reluctant to cooperate with the interview. When asked about this, Selene reported that she had experienced therapy in the past, "but it never worked." Selene reported that she was unmarried and living at in her own apartment with her boyfriend. During the initial sessions, Selene seemed to feel more comfortable discussing the substance use than other aspects of her life. Selene and I explored whether this was because that subject was well rehearsed during her recent in-patient treatment and prior substance abuse interventions. Selene made it clear that she understood that her substance use was because she "did not want to feel any emotions."

In subsequent sessions, Selene revealed that she had a 15-year history of self-harm, beginning when she was just ten years old because she "had a horrible self-image." Selene mentioned that she would engage in a range of activities including cutting and banging her head against a wall to the point of bleeding. Selene reported that her worst point was when she tried to kill herself by taking pills from the medicine cabinet (she did not know the nature of the medication).

Selene also reported that she has received four DUI's in the past five years. When asked how it could be possible that she still was allowed to drive, Selene responded that she was extremely compliant with all of the conditions placed onto her after each DUI. She would only do what was required to get herself released from the conditions set by the courts, before she would begin drinking and driving again.

Selene reported that she was raised by both parents and describes her childhood as "bad." Selene reported that she attended but did not graduate from an alternative high school. She later obtained her GED and currently works as a waitress in a local restaurant. Selene reported that she had a very unstable childhood, which included many people coming in and out of the household and exposure to lots of drugs and violence. She indicates that she feels her father acts as if he never grew up, stating, "he continues to operate as if he was an adolescent." Selene reported that she had been both physically and sexually abused throughout her childhood by her father. Selene mentioned that she believes this abuse began when she was about 6 years old and lasted until her father was incarcerated, when she was 11 years old. Selene mentioned that during this same period, her father would also "share" her with a friend of his in exchange for drugs.

Selene further stated that she witnessed her father sexually and physically abusing her younger brothers. She is the second oldest of five siblings, all of whom were removed from the home when she was 11 years old and placed in foster care when it was discovered that their father was molesting them. Selene and her older brother lived in a group home for 6 months before they were placed with their grandparents while Child Protective Services was investigating the allegations. Selene reported that her father was incarcerated for five years, beginning when she was 11 years old. When her father returned from prison, she was sixteen and had already moved out of the family home to live with her boyfriend.

Selene's substance abuse and mental health history were closely intertwined. Selene mentioned that her self-injurious behaviors escalated significantly when her father was removed from the household. She stated that she was confused about the emotions associated with the abuse and absence of her father and this triggered her attempts at self-harm. She also indicated that she felt that others blamed her for their father's removal form the house and the disruption of the family.

Selene reported that she was first sent to outpatient counseling following her abuse as a child. She stated she felt that this experience was pointless as there was already a lot of damage that had been done and her therapist did not seem to know how to deal with her. She recalls only attending a few sessions and not fully participating in the process. Selene mentioned that she has had one prior inpatient psychiatric admission a few years ago when she was feeling suicidal and had cut her wrist with a knife.

Selene reported that her substance use problems starting when she began sneaking alcohol from her parent's liquor cabinet. Soon after that, Selene began to smoke pot and use other drugs to get high so that she would not "feel any emotions." Selene reported to progressing in her drug use and eventually developing a heroin dependence which included her snorting daily for four years. She also reported smoking marijuana daily as well as heavy alcohol consumption during this same four-year period prior to getting into drug rehab. Selene mentioned that her substance use history included trying spice and cocaine a few times.

When asked about her adult relationships, Selene reported that she has always struggled with relationship issues, feelings of being worthless, wanting to give up, and suicidal thoughts. Selene confessed that she struggles with loving herself and feels that this relates to having had a troubled childhood that included physical and sexual abuse. Selene disclosed that she has a long history of "extreme love-hate relationships" stating that as a teen, she would agree to do things with any guy who would show interest in her. Selene confessed that she now realizes that she was struggling to cope with chronic feelings of emptiness and fear of rejection.

Selene reported that her ex-boyfriend mentally brainwashed her. She continued: "He was a drug dealer and a little bit older than I was and I was very impressed with how independent he was. I moved in with him at sixteen and was living a fairy tale life!" Selene confessed that she enjoyed the material things this lifestyle afforded her from such a young age and her boyfriend would travel back and forth with her between here and his hometown and they were treated like celebrities wherever they went. She admitted that the cost associated with this lifestyle was that she experienced physical and mental abuse from that same boyfriend. Selene recalled that this "fairy tale" lifestyle all came to a head when she was involved in a car accident at age twenty-three.

Prior to the accident, Selene reported that she had prior legal issues including being arrested for assault and for growing and selling pot. However, this time, she was charged with a DUI and for possession of a stolen firearm but stated that she committed neither offense. Selene clarified that her boyfriend was driving her car and she was in the passenger's seat. She added that she was having a bad reaction to something that she took at a party. Her boyfriend was driving her to get some help and he ran a red light and hit another vehicle. This caused their car to slide off the road and land in a ditch. She was unconscious in the passenger's seat when the ambulance arrived. They took her to the hospital, and she was placed in rehab for her overdose.

Selene stated that she assumed her boyfriend fled the scene because he did not have a driver's license and did not want to get arrested. She refused to cooperate with the police and denied that anyone else was in the vehicle at the time of the accident. As a result, she was charged for everything. After her fist stint in rehab, Selene returned to live in her family home. Her boyfriend had abandoned her and remained in hiding from the police.

At this point, her father was out of prison and back in the family home. Although the sexual abuse did not continue, Selene reported that her father was still actively abusing his pain medication and she felt her father was trying to get her to relapse. She stated that he would "lay a trail of breadcrumbs, like they do in the movies." Selene stated that her father is currently addicted to pain pills that he was prescribed for a back injury many years ago.

Selene reported that her father leaves his tin containing his pills that he has to take for the day laying around the house, unattended. She also reports finding single pills just lying on the floor or on a counter-top in places where they should not have been in the first place, including the bathroom inside her bedroom, or next to her yoga mat in the basement. She feels that he cannot stand the fact that she has gotten clean and has a secret desire to entice her to start using again.

Selene relayed that after several months of no contact with her ex-boyfriend and moving on with her life, she spotted her ex-boyfriend playing basketball in a park, while she was driving to work one day. She then saw him several more times at that location. After seeing him in that spot three times in two weeks, Selene reported that she began having recurring dreams about her sitting in the back seat of her own car and him driving with his current girlfriend in the front passenger seat. Selene related that this kind of out of control thing happened often in their relationship when she was getting high and her ex-boyfriend would have other women around and she felt powerless to control what was going on.

Selene reported that the drug dreams combined with the trail of breadcrumbs laid by her father proved to be too much for her and began to use again to disconnect from all of the emotions she was feeling. Her second overdose came very close to her one-year anniversary of her first overdose and Selene found herself back in rehab and starting her life all over again. After the second stint in rehab, Selene moved into a sober living environment. Selene realized that she could no longer live with her parents and moved all of her belongings out of her parental home. She reported that she continues to work to create new social groups and negotiated terms of a healthy relationship with her current boyfriend.

During a period when things seemed to have settled down a little for Selene and she was beginning to manage things well in her life, Selene came to a session visibly shaken. Selene arrived extra early for her appointment and I noticed her anxiously wringing her hands as she sat in the waiting room. As Selene entered the therapy room, I could hardly get my words out to ask how things were, before she blurted out that "Things are not good!" Selene confessed that she caught her current boyfriend sexting with another woman. She reported confronting him, but he denies cheating. She believes he has lied about so many things that she cannot believe him when he says he is not cheating.

Selene stated that she is frustrated with him because he has violated several of the conditions of his parole and believes it is only a matter of time before he is locked up again. She stated that she knows he has broken his sobriety by drinking alcohol, and he admits to selling marijuana although he denies smoking it. She is particularly concerned that he has begun to use heroin again despite actively attending NA meetings with her.

Selene stated that her ex-boyfriend would emotionally, psychologically, physically, and sexually abuse her. She claimed that he was very strategic, often finding creative ways to cause her physical pain without leaving any marks on her body that could be detected as signs of abuse. Her ex-boyfriend would host "sex parties for his top customers and she was frequently recruited into the drug-induced free-for-all. Periodically he would insult her in front of their friends by stating that having sex with her was "like throwing a hotdog down a hallway." Selene stated that she briefly lived in a house with her ex and his sister. They made her drive them around and would beat her up and her boyfriend would threaten to harm himself if she did not comply. She reported that her ex-boyfriend was "pretty high up" in a local gang and his sister would act as the enforcer and often threatened to put out a hit on her if she ever went to the police.

- Selene indicated that her ex-boyfriend's behavior was so abusive that it was difficult for her to determine the aspects of her current boyfriend's behavior that were problematic. She felt that as long as he was not doing the things that her ex did, her current boyfriend was, by default, a good guy. She was able to articulate that his behavior was bad for her and placed her at risk for relapse and self-injurious behavior but was frustrated with herself for not being able to set healthy limits and separate from him.

Selene reported that she has maintained her sobriety and resisted engaging in self-injurious behavior, up to this point. However, she has begun to engage in her self-injurious behavior (banging her head on a bannister post) after discovering that her boyfriend had been engaging in suspected cheating. Selene mentioned that she is even more concerned about her ability to stay sober as she has begun to have drug dreams again. Selene indicated that she was familiar with drug dreams and was more upset that the dream was about her ex-boyfriend. She stated that she had no interest in getting back with her ex-boyfriend and does not understand why he would show up in her dreams now.

Selene and I talked about the symbolism in the dream and that someone else driving her car with their current girlfriend in the passenger seat, while she was in the back seat may be connected to feelings of being out of control in her own life. We also talked about how the discharge paperwork from the hospital listed Selene as being diagnosed with several conditions related to her substance use, but there was more to this than meets the eye.

It was explained to Selene that the work with her was like peeling the layers of an onion. With each level of trust established, the more she disclosed an additional layer of trauma and family dysfunction. Selene indicated that she understood that in order for the therapeutic work to be effective and have a lasting impact, it would surely have to address the underlying issues that stem from her childhood abuse, and the long-term impact on her sense of self-worth. Selene agreed that she would benefit from examining the dynamics of how codependent personality traits manifest in her life and relationships and how she tends to unwittingly gravitate towards men who are stuck acting out the behaviors that result from their own childhood traumas (substance addiction and abuse, sex addiction, partner abuse, etc.) and unconsciously try to work through the broken relationships of their childhood.

I feel like it would have been hypocritical of me to only write about what I learned from the men I have worked with, and not report on what I learned from a reflection on my own experiences and behavior. In the section below, I outline some of the experiences which helped me to transform the way I look at relationships, and at my life.

CHAPTER EIGHT

Training Camp

"the naïve man often doesn't know that there is a being in him that wants to remain sick."

Robert Bly (2004)

Nature V. Nurture

After the memorial service for the last of my father's brothers to die, I was late in joining my two cousins at the bar for a drink to reminisce about our dearly departed dads. Although there are loads of cousins in our rather large extended family, the three of us share a special bond as we were born within eight months of each other. Only two of us grew up in New York, but we were shipped to the Washington, DC area to spend time in the summer at our uncle's house, where the third member of our trio resided. It was during these summers that we got into trouble together and the bonds of our kinship were solidified.

As I approached, my cousins were well into their conversation about their fathers and were concluding that their respective dad's inclination towards being players was in the genes. One cousin asserted that her half-brother stated that he has a healthy appetite for womanizing, and this was further proof that it was genetically predisposed for the men in our family to cheat. For the record, this notion that men are biologically wired to be unfaithful to their mates is not a theory that I endorse.

Although I have not been an angel, myself, I am willing to both admit to the wrong I have done, and more important, I am not going to try to explain it away by saying things like: "the devil made me do it" or "it was in my nature (and therefore I could not help it)." In fact, I believe that it is precisely that kind of thinking that lets men and boys off of the hook for their irresponsible, and often reckless behavior. It is also part of what allows those behaviors to continue.

When I reflect on my own family, it is striking to see how the behavior is defended, excused, and/or supported by both men and women. Case in point, my father and I once had a heated discussion about the behavior of his parents. It took place when my dad was already in his eighties and he had come to live with me as he was not fully capable of independently managing all of his daily responsibilities.

Because my dad no longer could see well enough to drive himself around, I became his chauffer. As much as I grumbled about the frequent weekend trips between

Baltimore and Washington, D.C., I secretly enjoyed myself because I would get to know my father and his siblings in a more honest and vulnerable way than my siblings ever did. They would often discuss things that were long held sibling secrets as if they had forgotten that I was in the room. All I had to do was to sit quietly, and I would learn lots! This trip to D.C. was no exception.

My father's much younger brother was recuperating from prostate surgery. My father and several other siblings went to visit my uncle on this particular day. They began to tease him stating that he had better take his time and fully recover because his younger girlfriend would want to have sex, once he got back home, and this may cause severe complications with his recovery. My uncle's response was swift and cutting: "That didn't stop the old man! I heard that mom threw the church aide out of the house during the recovery!" All five siblings erupted in laughter and continued their conversation with the nod of understanding that nothing more needed to be said about that topic.

During the car ride home, I asked my dad what my uncle meant. My father was strategic in his evasive techniques. He certainly did not owe me an explanation, and what was alluded to by my uncle, was none of my business. However, I was curious and the more I asked, the more my father talked in circles. Before I knew it, we had completed the hour-long drive home, and he still had not gotten to the point. He ended up saying that my grandmother was overly sensitive and that she had no reason to question her husband, the reverend. He then went on to state that his mother was known to be "reactionary."

I asked my father for clarification about the reactionary comment. He stated that his mother once caused a scene in front of the church. I asked about the circumstances that led to the altercation between a woman and my grandmother at the church. He replied that the woman was a widow and as the pastor of the church, it was grandfather's responsibility to check on the members of the congregation. He further stated that grandmother felt that grandfather spent too much time visiting that woman.

During that conversation, I stated that my grandmother had every right to confront the woman that her husband was having sex with. My father quickly interjected—"Nobody said anything about sex!" For a moment, he caught me off guard. He was right, I assumed sex was involved, but that "fact" was never disclosed. It took me a moment or two to recall that on the occasion of my father's eightieth birthday, someone was introduced to us that had the same last name as we did, and it turned out to be my father's half-sister from an "outside" relationship. I closed the conversation by reminding my dad that I met his half-sister at his eightieth birthday party, and adding that as far as I knew, people did not have kids back then without having sex.

I will admit that I had a bias in that conversation. After my mother died, I lived with my father's sister, who was the primary care giver for their elderly mother.

Having grown up in a house where my grandmother lived and not having a solid memory of my grandfather, who died when I was still very young, I was more than willing to give my grandmother the benefit of the doubt. What was strange to me, was that I felt that my father was willing to go out on a limb to cast his father in a good light and that included vilifying his own mother.

Another example was provided to me by my father's sister who raised me. She stated that it was important to marry a "good girl" and that I should not have sex with the woman I was interested in marrying until after we got married. She then went on to explain that the men in her generation were allowed to "sow their wild oats" and not sully the girls they would seek to marry. She gave the example that it was possible to use prostitutes for these purposes, while preserving the status of the good girls that were to be married. Now I acknowledge that they were raised in a different time and have a different set of values. They were born nearly 100 years ago and were raised by people who were born at the turn of that century. This was a very different generation.

I had a co-worker that was from my dad's generation. He was close to forty years older than I was and had been married for many years. He was also a social worker and I held a lot of respect for his insight and judgement, so I thought it would be a good idea to ask him for his advice when I realized that my marriage was in trouble. He responded by stating that my generation was too eager to think of separation and divorce as an option. He stated that his generation took their vows with more sincerity. He then stated that his formula for a successful marriage was to cheat on his wife each time he went away for a convention and by doing so they were able to have a successful marriage for all these years. I was disgusted. Maybe this was a value for people born in that generation, to stay married no matter what misery or infidelity. However, remaining married under such circumstances would not measure up to what I would call "successful."

I recall being about 13 years old and having a stroke of insight (or foresight) when I was celebrating having the phone numbers for about seven different girls and that one or more of those girls regarded me as her boyfriend. In that moment, I felt both successful and worried. Successful because the rules of the game in the city where I lived, and among the boys that were my friends clearly stated that this was success. It was a success that had eluded me for a long time, and now I could finally taste the beginning of what it was like to be a young player. Worried because, in that very moment I realized that as much fun as it was, this would not be good behavior to continue as an adult. For some strange reason, in my moment of success, I imagined how terrible it would be to behave this way, if I were married. I only wish I had exercised the discipline to consistently apply this insight.

Cheater's Convention Rules

During a recent session with a young married couple in their thirties, the wife was talking about how her husband had changed his routine, began using his phone to access porn websites as well as using prostitution and other "hook up" apps. He also began being "MIA" during pockets of the day. This was apparently a pattern of behavior that her husband displayed prior to their marriage but the behavior had dissipated for about a year before resurfacing. When confronted about his behavior during the therapy session, the husband admitted to visiting the websites and using the apps, but insisted that although he was tempted, by resisting the temptation, he was actually strengthening his ability to resist.

What happened next felt like he was trying to get the rest of the world to bend reality to meet his fantasy. He tried to get credit for his behavior (at least the behavior that he was willing to admit) by stating that by going to the websites and using the apps, without giving in to the act of having intercourse, was strengthening his resolve. It is almost laughable to note that I heard this same excuse deployed approximately one year earlier by another client in his fifties, who claimed that he knew the 900 numbers were a scam, but he was determined to call them so that he could "scam the scammers" but he received no gratification for the phone-sex and had no intention of cheating on his wife. I also heard similar nonsense when a couple in their forties came to see me after the wife discovered her husband's secret online dating profile.

Close to a century after my grandfather's transgressions, my father would attempt to deflect culpability by placing blame onto my grandmother by calling her "reactionary." Around that same time, my thirty-something year old client is deploying the same tactic to deflect from his own behavior by stating his wife was being "emotional" when reacting to his actions but all the while, he was taking zero responsibility for his own actions.

When I think about this, I am truly disappointed. A significant percentage of my practice includes couples work. Out of the couples, roughly 75% are seeking outside assistance in overcoming a break in trust that stems from an incident of cheating. I am disappointed that in the cases that deal with the men who are "suspected" of cheating, the stories I hear are virtually the same. What's worse, is that when cornered, the tactics that are employed are identical!

It seems as if there was a Cheaters Convention and the Executive Committee developed a set of rules regarding what to say and how to behave, if cornered. Similar to the training that members of the Armed Forces go through regarding how to conduct themselves if ever captured by enemy combatants, the Cheaters Convention created a clear-cut script and protocol of behaviors that were to be deployed under emergency circumstances.

The list of tactics includes, first and foremost, deny; next, change the subject; avoid eye contact; then give a blank stare; argue and claim that there is no proof; when presented with facts, claim that the facts are false; tell the other person that they are imagining things; go on the offensive, by accusing the other person of wrongdoing; get angry; use intimidation. Finally when all else fails, say that you are sorry (while still not admitting to anything) and say you will do better in the future, while having zero ideas on how to do that, which creates a very little possibility of fulfilling this hollow promise.

Protect the Harem

Contrary to what my cousin suggested; I am convinced that infidelity is not biologically determined. As a point of reflection, I asked myself, if not for nature, how the behavior could be so consistent over generations and for people who have never met one another. It also occurred to me to wonder what behavior or ideal was as consistent for women in the same way that this seemed to be consistent for men. That second question was easier to answer.

When I asked myself the question what is a consistent symbol for women, I came up with the notion of the white wedding dress. Research has shown that on average there are about 2.5 million weddings each year in the United States of America. I would estimate that as many as 80% of those have women getting married in the traditional (or some variation of) white wedding dresses. My belief is that this is a result of the Princess Fantasy that originated back in Victorian time.

This fantasy has a very strong hold on the imagination of many girls and remains with the vast majority of them throughout their lifetime and influences much that goes into the wedding day. This fantasy is the result of a set of some very strong symbols that have a binding hold on the consciousness of these women so much so that they believe it is something that they've always wanted instead of it being a desire that exists in society and was given to them; a conversation that existed in the world long before they were born, and then enveloped them soon after they gained a conscious awareness.

The question is what's the corresponding fantasy that has a hold on men that influences their behavior with as strong a resonance. In Boys Will Be Boys, Miriam Miedzian describes the stereotypical behaviors that are attributed to masculinity but are learned and practiced, more than they are biological. After my reflection, I thought of a comment that was made to me by an Assistant Professor of Social Work at University of Maryland that I met when I was an adjunct faculty member for the school. One afternoon when I showed up early to prepare for my class that evening, I encountered the professor as he was packing up his office and preparing to leave the university. I stopped and we chatted. When I asked him why he was leaving, he said he had been denied tenure and had to leave the post. I was surprised.

At that point in my career, I did not have a good handle on how tenure worked. It was all very confusing to me. From all that I could see, he was passionate about his teaching, professional in his conduct, and well-liked by his students and his colleagues. I told him that I did not understand how he, of all people, could not get tenure. He paused, and after some thoughtful reflection, he shared something with me that resonates to this day.

The professor stated that he joined a religious order from a very young age and did not spend a lot of time doing the typical things that boys would do while they grew up. As a result of his particular upbringing, he said he never learned how to "protect the harem." I thought it was an odd way to describe things, but he went on to clarify that he felt if he had learned to be more protective over the things that belonged to him, he would have been more successful in carving out a niche at the university. Although I have never heard anyone else use that sort of language to refer to how boys are socialized, similar to what happens to girls, for boys, there is a conversation that existed in the world long before they were born, and then enveloped them soon after they gained a conscious awareness.

If the princess fantasy (or queen archetype) governs the dreams of girls, then it is the king archetype that influences the dreams of boys. The king archetype as is represented in its various forms (king of the castle, head of the household, head of the family, head of the table, etc.) is a notion that permeates so much of our conscious and unconscious desires as men. We dream of being king and protecting the harem. However, we have no kingdoms, and as for the harems, they are not legitimate in societies where the practice is outlawed.

Being left without the ability to fulfil the four archetypes of the mature masculine (the king, the warrior, the magician, the lover), we spend our time stuck living out the shadow versions of our fulfilled existences. Specifically, one shadow of the lover archetype is the addicted lover, which Moore &

Gillette (1990) describe in King, Warrior, Magician, Lover, as "a collector of experiences, possessions, or women...without any structure, any overarching life philosophy, to connect the things he collects, his life feels fragmentary instead of whole. He is forever searching for the one thing, person, or experience that will make him feel truly alive."

Naivete

Many of my male clients say they want to change their behaviors (this is especially true for the ones that were brought in for couples therapy by their partners) but they quickly become vague when it comes to identifying the specific behavior that they wish to change and are well defended against admitting to any wrong doing. I often get the impression that they both want to change and simultaneously, want to continue the behavior that caused the problem. In Iron John, Robert Bly stated that "the naïve man often doesn't know that there is a being in him that wants to remain sick."

Bly goes on to say that "there is something in naivete that demands betrayal. The naïve man will have a curious link to betrayal, deceit, and lies. Not only will he betray others easily, being convinced his motives are always good, but when a woman lives with a truly naïve man for a while, she feels impersonally impelled to betray him. When there is too much betrayal around, the universe has no choice but to crystalize out some betrayal."

Numbness

Robert Bly also addressed the notion of Numbness, as he called it by stating that "a spiritual man may love light, and yet be entirely numb in the chest area." In response to a wound he received from his father, he felt that he could go to his mother for protection, but if he accepted that protection he would have to "learn how to feel as a woman feels. But I was a man, and so I decided to have no feelings at all". Bly continued and stated that his "head was fiery and full of blood, and my genitals were fiery and curious too. The area in between was the problem." He referred to the ability of his high school girlfriend to experience a range of emotions as a "spectrum of affection." In contrast, when he looked into his chest, he "saw nothing at all." Finally, he states that "it's possible that as a man gets older, certain numb parts of his body naturally begin to come to life."

Costs of the Game

It is painfully clear to me that there are costs that are associated with these behaviors. For me, those costs were counted as the loss of every romantic love relationship I ever entered. I can see now that my infidelity played out as a form of self-sabotage. A dear friend told me that they thought that I would never marry and would stay single because I did not seem like the "type."

I now understand that the commitment to this behavior (thinking it was normal, if not cool) kept me stuck in an adolescent mindset which left some parts of my emotional awareness underdeveloped. I am aware that this is also true for others who live the way that I once did. We never fully mature and remain stuck in a type of juvenile purgatory value of promiscuity.

   More important than our personal costs, is the collateral damage that we cause. There are the consequences of the denial. A century after my grandfather accused my grandmother to deflect from taking the blame for his own behavior, I still see men saying that it is the woman's fault for reacting to a man's bad behavior. I am sure that over time, this has an impact on the psyche of the women that are subject to the blame for the bad behavior of the men.

CHAPTER NINE

THE ALLEY MAN

> "Fighting on arrival, fighting for survival..."
> *Bob Marley*

   I spent too many years of my life being either angry or disappointed with my father and I am happy that we were able to make peace before he died. To some extent, I had buried my anger and engaged in some denial about the past until the day I received a call from his caregiver. She reported that he expressed his displeasure about how she prepared a meal for him by exhorting that: "you can ask Norma Beckles about the beating she got when she did not cook my rice properly!" I was surprised by the rage and pain that I instantly experienced as I heard from his caregiver that my father said in an almost boasting manner that he would beat my mother—over cooking rice!

   In that moment, I recalled the two men that my father was. In public he was so gentle, mannerly and considerate of others. He was so passive, that it seemed as if he was apologizing for his existence. While at home, he was a terrorizer to me, my brothers and sisters, and to our mom. I was confused! He seemed like two entirely different people. At first, this seemed like a contradiction. As I got older and learned a little bit about how the world works, I came to understand how this duality was possible.

My father was born in British Guiana in 1922. The whole world was different a century ago and for him, being a West Indian man of African ancestry, the son of a Moravian Minister, and raised as a British subject under colonial rule would create a toxic combination. The result is a three-part cocktail made up of the double consciousness that DuBois (1903) described in The Souls of Black Folk; mixed with what Blassingame (1972) outlined in The Slave Community as a bristling racial self-hatred that is handed down from one generation to the next; and seasoned with the violence that Fanon (1961) referred to in The Wretched of the Earth when he said "the colonized man will first manifest this aggressiveness which has been deposited in his bones against his own people." All of this, simmered in the heat of the equator, would manifest as a particularly austere form of passive-aggression to be meted out on my father's wife and children.

When I was about four years old, my family moved from the comfort, familiarity, and protection of our small community in New Amsterdam, Guyana, a small country on the northeastern tip of South America, to the

Brownsville section of Brooklyn, New York. Although we only lived at 1863 Park Place for three years, before moving to Queens, that time in Brownsville would come to have a major impact on my entire family.

I remember marveling as a child at how late the sun stayed up (before understanding that it was bright outside because of the streetlights). We were from a simpler place, during a simpler time and my parents thought it was safe to let their children play outside unsupervised and walk home from the bus stop, unescorted. Plus, with seven children, ranging in age from newborn to twelve, there was hardly any time to sit and watch.

On one evening, during an extended game of 'hide-n-seek' I strayed from the safe space in front of the brownstone where we lived and went around the bend in Park Place. I had a surprise encounter with a man that I will forever remember as "The Alley Man." He seemed to materialize in the entrance to the narrow passageway that led from the front to the back of adjacent buildings on the far side of our long city block. The tall slender man summoned me into the alley and without hesitation, I obeyed. This was well before the time of missing children on milk cartons and "Stranger Danger" slogans. This was a time of unquestioned obedience to adult authority. This was a time of…innocence.

The Alley Man instructed that I would have to lower my pants and squat close to the ground so the rats could smell my ass. He warned that I could not cry, nor be afraid, because the rats would smell the fear and bite me.

Most of all, he warned, that I could not tell, because rats could get into any house they wanted and if I told, they would come into my room at night when I slept and attack me. To this day, I cannot say exactly what else the Alley Man did in that alley. All I can recall is squatting there frozen, with my eyes closed, fearing the worst. To this day, I sleep with my head covered, as if the sheets could protect me from some nameless, faceless assailant.

I am clear that the meaning of what happened in that alley on that day has lingered with me for five decades. I was a victim. I felt vulnerable. I was afraid. My reaction was to freeze, squeeze my eyes tightly, and wait for the threat to pass. Then after the threat passed, the "contract" was to never talk about it again. My strategy for dealing with those feelings of vulnerability was to create a forcefield to protect the little boy from violation. The next tactic in my strategy was if I ever felt the threat of vulnerability, I would have to attack.

After only living in this country for six short years, my mother died from asthma-related complications. Losing her a few weeks before her 46th birthday caused a seismic shift in the universe for my family and for me, it landed in my psyche as the second crack in the arc of my personal evolution.

About *a year ago, I watched a TED MED Talk entitled: Childhood Trauma Lasts Forever*. This talk was presented by Nadine Burke Harris, MD, a pediatrician who clearly illustrated in her talk how adverse childhood experiences including such things as sexual abuse, parental mental illness, parental substance abuse, parental incarceration, parental separation and divorce, and domestic violence can profoundly impact the developing brains and bodies of children and ultimately impacts adult-onset disease. While I currently do what I can to engage in activities in an effort to address the physical implications of the adverse experiences of my childhood, it was a long time before I even had a sense that there would be psychological implications that needed to be addressed.

While reflecting on what was significant about her talk as it relates to physical disease, I thought about the implications for mental health. It almost goes without saying that childhood trauma negatively impacts mental health. In fact, we talk about it so much, in many instances, it has been relegated to the realm of "cliché" to quote a former client. However, I am not raising this point here, now, to recite the same tired worn out attempts to excuse bad behavior or to celebrate a diagnosis as badge of honor as some do at dinner parties. To the contrary, I am raising the point for the purpose of calling for the segment of our population who sense there is something wrong, but bury the trauma under a pile of denial, or, as that above-referenced client did, try to sidestep the significance of the impact of the trauma by stating things like: "I am a man, I am responsible for my actions. Whatever my father or mother did has nothing to do with this."

I will repeat in writing here the response I gave to my client when he raised his cliché objection: I do not deny anyone who chooses to take responsibility for their actions as an adult, in fact, I celebrate it. However, if you were raised by an alcoholic parent, had to go from door to door begging for food, had to run to the police to save your mother's life when she was being held at knifepoint, or were neglected, and then abandoned in an orphanage, those are the types of things that are traumatizing to the psyche of a child and have been known to manifest themselves in the kinds of problems around self-esteem, self-worth, relationships, and trust in adulthood that you are now experiencing. So, whether the tendency to "blame it on your mother" is a cliché or not, both the trauma you experienced in your childhood, and the psychological scars that it created -are real.

This tendency to "man up" and deny that something happened or that it had an impact is something I have seen in many of my male clients. It is noble, but often it is an obstacle that serves as a disconnect between the awareness of the dysfunction in which the adult male has engaged, and the understanding of the trauma that serves as the source of the pain, which fuels the dysfunction. This "self-made man myth" holds us back from our healing and has to be addressed before the real work can begin.

As for me, I have come to realize that my trauma and the strategy I developed in response to it came from all of the mental resources I could summon as a six-year-old kid. The residual effects of these combined incidents have impacted me in many areas of my life after those brief moments in that alley. The lasting damage from those moments in the alleyway and the embodiment of my response manifests as anger, aggression, problems with trust, and infidelity, to name a few.

Behind Closed Doors and Beneath the Surface

It took me a long time to realize that despite how much I detested it, I had embodied the same duality to my personality that I saw in my father. Many people described me as a kind and patient dad and a good catch. On occasion, I would chuckle inside and say to myself, if they only knew. I knew I had a temper, but there was nothing like coming face to face with the understanding of how others respond to you when they see you at your worst. One night, my first son woke up from a nightmare, crying. When I was comforting him and asked what's wrong, he said: "I dreamed that you were a monster with big teeth and red eyes." My heart broke…I was his monster. No matter how much I loved my children and was willing to sacrifice for their wellbeing, there was something else that I was showing them through my angry outbursts, and it began to surface in their nightmares.

My heart broke a second time when my younger son, then an adult, began losing work because he could not control his temper. He was getting beaten up because he could not control his outbursts. He had gotten locked up and was facing a felony assault charge because he felt violence was a viable option for resolving a personal conflict. I shudder to think that I could have buried this "secret" by not talking about it, but it still came out to play. Avoiding the anger was no longer enough. I knew I had to do something to resolve it.

Basic Flaw

"I never meant to confuse you. Never meant to complicate your life. For loving matters of the heart. Being stuck in a triangle of emotion. It's one thing to want somebody. Another thing to need somebody. And another thing to love somebody. All I know is that I love you. Love you like you love him. Like I've never loved another."
         Raheem DeVaughn (2015)

My heart broke a third time when she said: "You are still not living your truth. You spend so much time trying to appear like you are good, that you fail to have any time left to spend actually doing good. This is the same reason you have trouble finding fulfillment at work and this is the reason we cannot be together." The woman I refer to as my spiritual bride was sounding the death knell for our relationship and any chance of a future reconciliation. It was as if she had some special x-ray vision and could see into my soul; as if she knew things about me that I could not yet find words to express.

During those conversations, I struggled to understand the full meaning of her words. They felt like both an accusation and a condemnation. It made me think of the scene from A Color Purple where Celie says: "Until you do right by me, everything you even think about is gonna crumble!" (Walker, 1992). I felt as if a sexy witch was casting a spell that doomed me to be trapped in a pattern of failed relationships for the rest of my life if I did not answer the question—what is my truth?

My truth is that I was sneaky and would lie to conceal my insecurity so that others would not find out the truth. I have used my intellect and humor to keep people off balance and at bay so that no one would get close enough to notice. With her, I let my guard down and she got close enough to see that I was still hiding something. With her, this was the closest I ever got to my Thrive Principle. During our interactions, I was able to access my Bliss Level and I consistently resonated on my highest thinking, laughing, and loving. When I was with her, I was my best self. I was home.

I thought that all of the scars were healed over. I thought I was okay. I spent so much time helping people through their stuck places, only to learn way too late that my flaw was buried so deeply that I never saw how it impacted my self-esteem. This was a big piece of what I was hiding, and it eroded the very foundation of our relationship. When she asked me what I was hiding, I panicked, and ran away, emotionally. I used the tried and true tactics of deflection, and the counter-attack to keep the focus off of me.

> *"I was a man with no purpose, with no one to love, and no one to love me, but for me."*
> *Lionel Ritchie (1976)*

I ran so far away from home that I feel that I have been lost meandering through the wilderness. I thought that I left the best part of me with her and that she held the key to fix what was wrong with me. All I needed was for her to tell me what she saw when she looked into my soul and how to fix whatever it was that was broken in there. It took some time, but I eventually realized that there had been no "spell" cast on me, and she was not going to "fix" me. I needed to do my work and based on the places where I knew I was stuck, and the other places where I had blind spots, it would only be through doing my work that I could grow and have a chance at a more fulfilling life.

As I mentioned in my earlier work, *Crossing the Desert*, my work with the many men who were locked up for their inability to properly identify, articulate, and express their emotions led me to see the similarities that existed between them and the men in my family. Likewise, my work with men in general, and in particular, men who were coming in with their partners for couples counseling, I again saw similarities. Much of the upset and difficulty the couples were experiencing stemmed from a fundamental disagreement in the definition of what constituted cheating.

On the surface, it would seem like it was a difference of opinion between the men who were suspected of cheating and their partners. The simple solution to this would be to clear up the misunderstanding and everybody would go home happy. When I began to look closely at this issue, I realized that there were some patterns emerging. For many of the men, there seemed to be a reluctance to "understand" that there would be a problem with the types of things they were doing and a strong resistance to doing anything differently.

Seeing the impasse between these partners in a

relationship time, after time, because of the same things let me see clearly exactly why my relationship got stuck at that same impasse and that without changing some very specific things about my behaviors (and beliefs) I could never fully participate in a fulfilling romantic relationship.

I recall that when verbally jousting with a person and wanted to say I disagreed with them in a playful way, I would say: "I used to think the way you do, but then I changed my mind." I came to understand that I had to change my mind (my perceptions, my attitudes, and my beliefs) about fundamental concepts in two very specific ways. The first was that I had to change my mind about what I deserved and what I was willing to accept (or not).

I realized that I had been holding onto a secret. This secret existed as a knowing, which resided in me below the level of my consciousness. It was a deep-seeded belief that something within me had been damaged during the traumas. This secret belief was that fundamentally, I had a flaw, and that I would never be good enough. This belief that something was broken, that I was broken, led me to do many things, for most of which, I am not proud. I did not have to look very far for clues. One such clue was my attraction to emotionally unavailable women as was evidenced by the number of relationships I had with married women.

At first, I thought it reflected some difficulty that I had with commitment. This was certainly true, but when I saw how much pain I would experience when it became clear that because these women were already married to someone else, they could never truly allow themselves to be fully available to me, I realized how foolish and lonely I was destined to be. I had no idea that I could stoop so low. I was pained when I had to face the degradation and hurt that I was willing to accept because I saw that my choices would lead to me falling in love, but never being able to get that love back.

The second thing that I had to change my mind about was what I was willing to do (or not do). I had to admit to myself that there was all manner of things that I was willing to do and then go to elaborate extremes to tell myself it was okay. Before I changed my mind, it was acceptable to engage in all manner of duplicity including both consciously and subconsciously to engage in behavior that would sabotage my marriage and subsequent "committed" relationships.

I was willing to engage in flirtatious phone conversations with a female co-worker, while I was engaged to be married. In a separate incident, I was willing to take the dog for a walk and hold hands with someone that I believed was only a friend, again, while still engaged to my fiancée. My duplicity included that I was willing stop in a jewelry store to get the phone number from a complete stranger, while I was not only married, but on the way home from visiting my wife in the hospital after the birth of our second child. What's more, I was willing to make a clandestine arrangement to meet a co-worker in a secret location, have her disrobe, kiss, fondle and attempt intercourse with her. I was able to do all of this while married and justify to myself that I was not cheating because the session ended without climax because I felt guilty and lost my erection.

By being willing to face the truth about each of these two issues, I was able to see that there was a deep disconnect between what I was willing to show the world and what I was allowing myself to do. This disconnect stemmed from a deep-seeded sense of wounding to my self-esteem and a willingness to live outside of integrity, which, in and of itself left me spinning rapidly through cycles of shame, guilt, deceit, secrecy, pain, enmity, etc. I became vividly aware of the fact that I was spending lots of time attempting to look good, but very little time was spent engaged in the actions required to actually be what I thought a good person was. As a result, despite how "good" I may have looked, deep down inside, I felt like an imposter.

Originally, I thought that my actions were ego syntonic. I was behaving based on the pleasure principle, the more things that I did that felt good, the better it was for my ego. I did not think of myself as a bad guy and I was able to find ways to tell myself stories to justify the often unacceptable and occasionally deplorable things that I did. However, at a deep and fundamental level, I knew that what I was doing was wrong and I would feel guilt and shame afterwards. The truth is that by having my energy regularly vibrating on the lower levels of guilt and shame I was actually damaging my sense of self-worth, my self-image, and my self-esteem.

This work began with me telling the truth to myself.

This was the hardest part. I thought of myself as a nice guy and I presented that image to the world and interacted with the world by exchanging in a currency based on that premise. On one hand, I can imagine that there are aspects of my behaviors that can be linked to my past traumas. On the other hand, while I certainly take responsibility for all of my actions and the pain that they caused, there is something else that comes to mind. As I think of the male clients whose behavior shows some similarities to my own, I am led to believe that there are some elements of our upbringing that allow us to believe that these behaviors are acceptable and defendable.

CHAPTER TEN

THE ANTIDOTE

> I was locked inside
> A prison of my own design
> Every wall was painted grey...
> *Memphis by Cassandra Wilson (1995)*

My premise when I decided to write this book was that I wanted to write a teaching memoir which highlighted the lessons I learned over the past thirty years or more while working with men who have struggled with their maladjustment and readjustment to the hands that life has dealt them. The thesis in the book is pretty simple: All people are born with a mission or purpose to fulfill. James Hillman calls this our soul's code. Although Hillman writes in his book, The Soul's Code, that our souls are accompanied on the journey that is our lifetime with a guide to help ensure that we fulfill the mission, there are obstacles that may still impede our progress.

Our ability to fulfill that mission is based on our personal evolution to our highest level of functioning. This requires reaching adulthood in all of our capacities: physical, emotional, psychological, spiritual, and logical.

The goal then becomes to assist men to evolve beyond the places where they are stuck on the arc of their personal evolution. We have to break down the barriers to reach male vulnerability and identify where they are along the spectrum of emotional well-being. The spectrum, which ranges from emotional mutism through emotional intelligence and extends up to emotional fluency. From the lowest level of functioning described as "soul murder" to the highest level of fulfillment where our soul resonates with the soul of the world.

Some adult men remain trapped in child-like behaviors that were learned in what I referred to as the Training Camp in chapter 8. Unfortunately, despite the progress that has been made, there continues to exist a set of arcane notions about what it means to be a man, that serve as a standard by which our society limits the emotional evolution of boys and we now have a stage of prolonged adolescence, or at least the valuing of adolescent-like activities which stretches out for a full two decades, or longer.

In *Guyland: The perilous world where boys become men,* Michael Kimmel (2008) asserts that by discouraging boys from showing emotions or admitting to weakness, we curtail their emotional development. He goes on to say that "the passage between adolescence and adulthood has morphed from a transitional moment to a separate life stage. Adolescence starts earlier and earlier, and adulthood starts later and later."

Adverse Childhood Experiences (ACEs) negatively impact our growth and development toward full maturity in one or more of our capacities. Although the adverse experience may not rise to the level of soul murder, research into ACEs well documents their impact throughout the lifespan of the individual. The effects of these trauma are that they skew our perspective and limit our functioning. In response to the experience, we develop a way of being that is predicated on the perspective that we had at the time of the trauma. For example, if we experienced a major trauma at age six, we experience what I call a crack in the arc of our personal evolution. Often the Arc of your Personal Evolution is fractured when the natural growth and development is interrupted by trauma.

As a result, we develop a sort of 'psychic scar tissue' around this crack and our ability to respond stops evolving in that particular capacity and our reaction to similar types of threats seems to be informed by the perspective we had at the time of the original trauma. In other words, if we experience an emotional trauma at six years old, our psyche develops a response from the perspective of a six-year-old. Later in life, when we see similar threats, our default reaction rises to the surface. We may be an adult and use adult words, but our reaction is being informed from a vastly different aspect of our personality. Unfortunately, the tools that were developed from the perspective of a six-year-old would hardly be adequate (or acceptable) for use by an adult.

For many of my clients, these cracks exist along the emotional spectrum at the level of guilt, shame, and denial. Even when we rise to resonate at the level of anger, which is higher than the three emotional responses listed above, it is still only in the lowest quartile of the emotional spectrum. If we are to move higher up on this spectrum of emotional existence, we have to become free of the emotional prison that these psychic scars have formed. When our emotional response is generated from these base level emotions, our emotional baseline becomes anchored in this zone. In order to be capable of different range of emotional responses, we must learn how to regularly resonate in a vastly different emotional zone. This will free us from the prison.

In Care of the Soul, Thomas Moore (1998) asked "Why does our culture seem so angry at things?" He then goes on to offer a possible reason by stating "One reason may be that we are cut off from soul." He goes on to state that "there is no separation between our soul and the soul of the world."

When we consider the levels of consciousness, we can see it along a continuum that ranges from evolved and resonating at the highest level, the *Bliss Level of Consciousness* to regressed and resonating at the Base Levels of Consciousness, where people who act out their frustration on themselves or others.

Moore stated that if we are to achieve harmony with our internal conflicts and restlessness, what Jung refers to as the divine union, it will require striking a balance between the "ambition, fanaticism, fundamentalism, and perfectionism" of spirit and the "soupy moods, impossible relationships, and obsessive preoccupations" of soul. Robert Bly refers to the importance of balance in Iron John, which is about finding a middle path between the greater awareness of the 'sensitive new age guy', and the power and vitality of the warrior.

The ACEs that caused the damage to the psyches of the men and women portrayed in this book has been described by Shengold as soul murder. Correspondingly, the remedy would be found in what Thomas Moore described in Care of the Soul as "looking out for things, noticing how and where they are suffering, seeing their neuroses, and nursing them back to health." My work with my clients is to assist them in doing the work to bring their souls back to health. In that sense, I feel that I am a Soul Warrior.

It is important to understand that the conversation has been in the world before you were born and if you are to be effective in changing the situation that is manifesting the problems in your life, you must employ different strategies than the ones you have tried before. In order to change the conversation, you will have to change the thinking. However, you may also need to examine the company you keep and see if those conversations support the new conversation, you seek to create.

Bliss Level of Emotional Vibrations

Many of my clients grew up in families that transacted an emotional currency of shame, guilt, fear, anger, apathy, blaming, scapegoating, judgement, etc. Often a client would come in for therapy to deal with depression, anxiety, substance abuse, or some other factor that tipped their life out of balance. However, when the symptoms were relieved, the client would have climbed out of crisis or victim mode, simply to return to vibrating on an emotional level that was familiar. This emotional vibrational level is what they have grown accustomed to after a lifetime of practice. Though the level may be familiar, it may not necessarily be healthy. In his best-selling book, The Happiness Advantage, Shawn Achor, put it best: "You can eliminate depression without making someone happy. You can cure anxiety without teaching optimism" (2010).

The first step in creating a healthy mental and emotional environment is to become aware of the role you are playing to keep things stuck where they are. Then if you find that the environment that you have been maintaining does not suit you, satisfy you, or help you get to where you say you want to go, you get to choose what you will do about it.

A review of several emotional vibrational frequency charts consistently displayed a scale of consciousness that ranges from shame to enlightenment. In Power vs Force, Dr. David Hawkins segments the scale of consciousness into three separate categories. He stated that everything that calibrates between 0 and 200 on the scale makes the body go weak; everything above 200 makes the body go strong; and having a frequency of 500 or above means that we are in harmony with our body and our environment (2014).

The emotions that are registered at the lower vibrations consist of fear, grief, apathy, guilt, and shame. I call this grouping the Victim Level. The middle group of emotional vibrations include desire, anger, pride, courage, neutrality, acceptance, and reason. I call this the Survivor Level. Then the Upper vibrations resonate around Love, Joy, Peace, and Enlightenment. I call this the Bliss Level.

For a significant percentage of the clients on my caseload, anger, shame, and guilt were virtually their constant companions, prior to coming in for therapy. Experience has demonstrated that when the victim level emotions are waiting, just outside the psychological door, ready to pounce, it becomes difficult to consistently entertain healthier levels of emotional vibrations. When we anchor our level of emotional vibrations on the victim level, this becomes our baseline. However, when we elevate our level of emotional vibrations on a regular basis, we move ever closer to creating a new baseline. When we practice elevating our emotional vibrations to resonate around love, joy, peace, enlightenment, and other top-level emotions, we are accessing the *Bliss Level.* By accessing the Bliss Level with intention, on a daily basis, we establish it as the new baseline for our internal psychological and emotional climate.

Cultivating the Principle of Thrive

Around the time when my heart broke the third time after being told by my sweetheart that I was not living my truth, I realized how much I felt as though I was in conflict with my entire existence. I had just lost the love of my life, I had been recently fired from my job, I was trying (unsuccessfully) to influence my son's life in a direction that I thought was best for him, and the city I had been working the past two decades to improve, had just erupted in riots. So many of the things that I stood for and held dear were out of balance.

I was confronted with the notion that I could not control those outcomes and maybe it would be best if I stopped trying to control them. I felt the need to regroup. This was the launch of a season of letting go. I sold just about all of my worldly possessions—my extensive collection of books, and a wonderful array of music, which I had been collecting for over thirty years. I sold my car, most of my clothes, and anything else that I could not carry with me on the plane. I bought a one-way ticket to Ecuador, and within two-weeks of making the decision, I was settling into my room in the hostel in downtown Manta.

I was determined to have a new beginning. *The Alchemist* by Paulo Coehlo was the only book that I kept, and although I had read it before, I chose to read it a second time. After rereading the Alchemist in in a small fishing town on the northwest coast of Ecuador, I got very clear that, like the main character in the book, my treasures did not have to be acquired in a far-away land.

As in *The Alchemist*, my search for peace and fulfilment took me to far-away lands and through a clarifying process. I also went through a purging of the illusion that something was better in South America that; something was going to be better somewhere else. Similar to the pilgrimage that was taken in *The Alchemist*, I had to go way to find that my treasure, and beauty, and peace were actually back home.

While away, I was able to sort things out for myself and fully reflect on a notion that I had wrestled with for years. Several years before, I came to the realization that despite society's effort to shift the language from victim of (fill the blank) trauma to survivor of said trauma, we did not go far enough. I celebrate the movement that has freed so many people from the language of victim. However, I firmly believe that each time we proclaim that we are a survivor of any trauma, the simple action of naming the trauma, is, in and of itself, a tether that connects our present-day sub-consciousness to that trauma of many years ago.

Although there are those who would argue with me, as if my suggestion that they didn't use the word survivor, somehow implies that they did not survive. To the contrary, I am completely in support of everyone doing the work they need to do to get their lives into a healthy state. I am merely suggesting that there is something beyond surviving that is possible. My point simply is that as we consciously or sub-consciously hold onto the label of the trauma in how we identify ourselves, we limit our ability to go beyond surviving and get into the domain of thriving.

Entering the domain of thriving does not happen simply because we right a wrong or fix something that was broken. Thriving does not kick in just because we get back to so called normal, or as Achor put it: "If all you strive for is diminishing the bad, you'll only attain the average and you'll miss out entirely on the opportunity to succeed." Thriving becomes possible when we activate our consciousness and behaviors to engage in the activities that symbolize thriving for us. This is the *Principle of Thrive*.

The *Principle of Thrive* would vary from person to person. What constitutes thriving for me would be different from what constitutes thriving for you. With particular clients, I invite them to embark on a journey to discover what their lives would look like if they would activate the Principle of Thrive into their personal circumstance. For those clients who are open to the exploration, I work with them to cultivate the right combination of factors that would be necessary for them to thrive within their lives.

Sometimes this can be as simple as noticing the beauty that exists in your daily existence; appreciating the loving support that's provided by your partner; maintaining a solid emotional boundary around your home; protecting your emotional and psychological space from negative external forces and keeping it sacred. It may be necessary to disconnect from the conversations, experiences, and relationships that harken back to the mindset of victim.

At a minimum, the primary components of the Principle of Thrive would be cultivated by weeding the garden in relation to your relationship with self (self-talk); your relationship with others (the company you keep); your destination (where do you want your life to go); and how you embrace the work that you do (doing work that feeds you in how many ever ways you need to be fed). An important distinction is the one between noble profession and right livelihood. Many people believe that the only way to live a good life is to work in a noble profession. However, once one is committed to living a right livelihood, then it matters less about the work you do; it's the peace that you cultivate while you do it.

For the purpose of this conversation, I have included as an example, the components that come together to form the Principle of Thrive for me. I have established a personal manifesto (which includes my personal mission, personal vision, and personal value statements) and I recite each day before I leave the house. I intentionally keep my soul in the company of good souls for as high a percentage of the time as possible. Additionally, I am committed to being cause in the effect of laughter for both others and myself as a very essential component of the deliciousness of my life. I maintain my Bliss Level by what I affectionately refer to as living in the GAP. At least twice each day, I intentionally bring my emotional awareness to resonate on the vibrations of gratitude, abundance, and peace (GAP).

I have managed to identify the perfect balance for me by engaging in work that has meaning because it allows me to contribute to the growth and development of others. Now that I have activated the Principle of Thrive in my life, I use my work to facilitate the process through which others can activate that within their lives.

My work now focuses on helping my clients to move along the emotional continuum from emotional mutism to emotional fluency; to activate the Thrive Principle within their lives and to create practices to regularly access the Bliss Level of emotional vibration. In my Soul Warrior Inception Matrix Workshop, I help clients to identify what their specific ACES were, how they coped with them, how that holds them back today, and how to evolve their psychological tool kit. In short, I challenge my clients to move beyond merely surviving and to begin thriving. I celebrate them, when they take the challenge, in the same way that I now offer you to take the challenge with this simple phrase: Welcome to the WORK!

BIBLIOGRAPHY

Achor, S. (2010) The Happiness Advantage: How a positive brain fuels success in work and life. New York: Currency.

Beckles, W. (1996) Mood Music (unpublished manuscript). Baltimore, MD.

Beckles, W. (2006) Crossing the Desert: One Man's Journey from emotional mutism and life in exile to becoming whole. Baltimore, MD: Sunny House Press

Beckles, W. (2010) Smashing the Gap: The BASIC system for academic success. Baltimore, MD: Sunny House Press

Blassingame, John W. (1972) The Slave Community: Plantation life in the antebellum south. Oxford University Press

Bly, R. (2004) Iron John: A book about men. Boston, MA: Da Capo Press.

Chapin, H. (1974). Cat's in the Cradle [Recorded by Harry Chapin]. On Verities [Album]

Clinton, G. (1982). Atomic Dog [Recorded by George Clinton]. On Computer Games [Album]

Coelho, P. (1988) the Alchemist. San Francisco, CA: Harper Collins.

DeVaughn, R. (2015). All I Know [Recorded by Raheem DeVaughn]. On Love, Sex, Passion [Album]

DuBois W.E.B. (1903) The Souls of Black Folk: Essays and sketches. Chicago, A. G. McClurg.

Fannon, F. (1961) The Wretched of the Earth. New York: Grove Press.

Hawkins, D. (2002) Power vs. Force: The hidden determinants of human behavior. Carlsbad, CA: Hay House

Hendrix, H. (1988) Getting the Love You Want: A guide for couples. New York: Henry Holt and Company.

Hillman, J. (1996) The Soul's Code: In search of character and calling. New York: Ballentine Books

Hillman, J. (1979) The Dream and the Underworld. New York: Harper Collins.

Hucknall, M. & Moss, N. (1985). Holding Back the Years [Recorded by Simply Red]. On Picture Book [Album]

Jung, C. G. (1959) Four Archetypes. Princeton, NJ: Princeton University Press.

Jung, C. G. (1990) The Undiscovered Self. Princeton, NJ: Princeton University Press.

Kalsched, D. (2013) Trauma and the Soul: A psycho-spiritual approach to human development and its interruption. London: Rutledge.

Kimmel, M. (2008) Guyland: The perilous world where boys become men. New York: Harper Collins.

Kimmel, M. (2013) Angry White Men: American masculinity at the end of an era. New York: Nation Books.

Marley, R. & Williams, N. (1984). Buffalo Soldier [Recorded by Bob Marley]. On Legend [Album].

Mate, G. (2010) In the Realm of Hungry Ghosts: Close encounters with addiction. Berkeley, CA: North Atlantic Books.

Moore, R. & Gillette, D. (1990) King Warrior, Magician, Lover: Rediscovering the archetypes of the mature masculine. New York: Harper Colins.

Moore, T. (1998) Care of the Soul: How to add depth and meaning to your everyday life. New York: Harper Collins.

Real, T. (1997) I Don't Want To Talk About It. Overcoming the secret legacy of male depression. New York: Scribner

Ritchie, L. (1976) Just to be Close to You [Recorded by The Commodores]. On Hot on the Tracks [Album]

Shengold, L. Soul Murder (1989): The effects of childhood abuse and deprivation. New Haven, CT: Yale University Press.

Shengold, L. (1999) Soul Murder Revisited. New Haven, CT: Yale University Press.

Walker, A. (1992). The Color Purple. London: Women's Press

Wilson, C. (1995). Memphis [Recorded by C. Wilson]. On New Moon Daughter [Album].

ABOUT THE AUTHOR

Dr. Wayne Beckles is a therapist, author, educator, and sought-after public speaker. He is a licensed certified clinical social worker with three decades of practice experience in the field of mental health. His clinical practice includes providing psychotherapy in multiple settings including outpatient mental health settings, group practices, and maximum-security settings where he examined the lasting impact of childhood traumas on adult behavior and developed his model the Soul Warrior Inception Matrix. Dr. Beckles has authored several works including: Redefining the Dream: African American Male Voices on Academic Success; Crossing the Desert: One Man's Journey from Emotional Mutism and Life in Exile to Becoming Whole; and Smashing the Gap: The BASIC System for Academic Success.

Dr. Beckles is an Associate Professor of Social Work at Cecil College and runs a private practice with offices in Oxon Hill and Bel Air, Maryland where he works with individuals and couples. He holds a Doctor of Education from *Morgan State University*; a Master of Arts from the University of Chicago; and a Bachelor of Science from Stony Brook University. He has a quick sense of humor and finds ways to incorporate laughter into his clinical practice. He prefers activities that engage the mind and spends his free time reading, listening to music, and enjoying a good movie.

www.drwaynebeckles.com

291019-100-1-60W